Just Add Buddha!

Just Add Buddha!

Buddhist Solutions for Hellish Bosses, Traffic Jams, Stubborn Spouses, & Other Annoyances of Everyday Life

Franz Metcalf

Ulysses Press

Questions on page 104 are from page 68 of *The Lazy Woman's Guide
to Just About Everything*, by Judie O'Neill and Bridget Fonger
(Elephant Eye Press, 2001).

The quote on page 143 and the translation on page 152 are © 2003
Taigen Dan Leighton, reprinted with permission from pages 142 and
180 of *Faces of Compassion: Classic Bodhisattva Archetypes and
Their Modern Expression* (Wisdom Publications: 199 Elm Street,
Somerville, MA 02144; www.wisdompubs.org).

The two haiku on pages 138 and 139 are reprinted with permission
from Salon.com.

Published by: Ulysses Press
        P.O. Box 3440
        Berkeley, CA 94703
        www.ulyssespress.com

Library of Congress Control Number 2004101018
ISBN 1-56975-409-8

Printed in Canada by Transcontinental Printing

10 9 8 7 6 5 4 3 2

Editor: Richard Harris
Design: Leslie Henriques, Sarah Levin
Editorial and production: Lily Chou, Claire Chun

Distributed by Publishers Group West

To my mother and father,
who have shown me such compassion and wisdom,
and to all the later bodhisattvas in my life,
whose gifts fill these pages,
I dedicate the merit of this book.

Table of Contents

Acknowledgements

*"Innumerable labors brought us this book,
the gift of many living things."*

I adapt these words from the Zen Buddhist meal blessing as I reflect on the long process of creating what you now hold. No book is separate from a whole throng of living beings.

In celebration of this particular book's coming into being, and on its behalf, I give thanks for the efforts of Ray, Leslie, Bryce, Lynette, Claire, and many others at Ulysses Press who fostered it from the beginning. I praise the surgical speed and lucid simplicity of Richard Harris, who cleaned it up. I am deeply grateful for the contributions of Taigen Daniel Leighton Sensei, Sumi Loundon, Philip Goldberg, Mardi Horowitz, and Judie O'Neill and Bridget Fonger, who manifest themselves visibly on the pages that follow. My live-in teacher Nina Ruscio, my beloved, my *sine qua non*, also manifests herself here, and no words will ever comprehend my gratitude for her. Finally, I bow to Rinban Noriaki Ito, Professor Daniel Capper, Jason Siff, and various members of the Forge Guild of Spiritual Leaders and Teachers, whose manifestations in this book are invisible, but pervasive.

More largely, I celebrate the trees, plants, and animals that provided this book's paper, ink, and binding glue; the hundreds of people who wrote the software, and made, marketed, and delivered the computers on which it was written; the printers who turned bytes into books; the folks in the distribution system who brought these books to your store (or door); the people working in that store who connect you to the worlds of words; and, finally and fundamentally, you who read this. Without your hunger—without your *demand*—for a richer life, this book would not exist.

I acknowledge and thank you all.

More formally, I thank Salon.com for permission to reprint the two wonderful haiku on pages 138 and 139. You can find the originals and many others at http://archive.salon.com/21st/chal/1998/ 02/10chal2.html (and /10chal3.html). I thank Judie O'Neill and Bridget Fonger for the penetrating (!) questions from their practical and delightful *The Lazy Woman's Guide to Just About Everything*. And I thank Taigen Dan Leighton for the quote and translation from his luminous *Faces of Compassion: Classic Bodhisattva Archetypes and Their Modern Expression*. Both these books are immensely helpful; buy them and see for yourself.

Nine bows!

INTRODUCTION:
Starting Where You Are

ESTEEMED READER, I MUST tell you right away that I don't think profound spiritual teachings are helpful for most of us. I'm serious. Regular people need regular practices, not virtuoso ones. Regular practices are the root of Buddhism. That's why I love Buddhism. That's why I love this book.

Since I'm a regular person, living in the real world, I've written this book to be real and helpful. It's not for devotees of exotic doctrines or advanced practices. It contains no secret teachings for initiated acolytes. Rather than revealing how to get to nirvana in eight easy jhanas, this book is all about getting through the day a little bit happier.

This is a book for spiritual beginners (which is most of us) and for more advanced spiritual types who can use a refresher now and then (which is pretty much everyone else). It's for those of us who don't have frequent visions of universal oneness, who weren't Tibetan monks in our past lives, who can't tell their kundalini from their cannelloni. We know who we are; we're the salt of the earth. We're our kind of folks!

Yet I call you "esteemed reader"—because you deserve it. After all, here you are checking out this Buddhist book. Good for you. Inwardly you may be thinking, "Despite my innumerable failures, I still know I can make some spiritual progress." Damn right you can! You just need someone to speak to you on your level. This is where I come in. I know that level well.

This book is called *Just Add Buddha* because "just add Buddha" emphasizes our power to add excellence to our lives, right now. It's about progress and moments, not perfections and permanence. This entire book celebrates a level of practice some serious Buddhists call "shallow," but to be nicer to ourselves, we'll use the equally correct term, "fundamental."

Let me repeat something absolutely . . . well . . . fundamental: I wrote this book because fundamental practices are what you need, and they're what I do. You need them; I've got them. Sure, there are plenty of Buddhist books describing rarified meditation techniques, transcendent compassion exercises and so on. And there are many wonderful, qualified teachers who can embody these things for you, live the deep spirituality of the Buddha right in front of you, and push you to share in it yourself. If you want to read those books and study with those people, I bow to you. I deeply respect you. I wish you glorious success. Now, off to the monastery with you!

For everyone who's still with me, here's what I've got. I'm happy to share.

Fundamental Practice

You'll see fundamental practice unfold in all its lack of glory as you read this book. Here's a basic definition: fundamental practice is what anyone can do, right now, to make her or his life excellent. It's practice from the bottom up, and nothing is too basic to be included. Fundamental practice is not necessarily easy, but it's always possible. Fundamental practice is what leads—the fates willing!—to deep practice. Fundamental practice is faking it so that later it comes naturally. Fundamental practice is that pasted-on smile that makes the real one come more easily. Fundamental practice is the steps you take when you can't find the end of the path on the map—when you can't even read the map, when you don't even have a map. Fundamental practice leads directly to awakening. Fundamental practice is the holy life.

This is a book of "as if." Dale Carnegie once said, "Act as if you were already happy and that will tend to make you happy." He didn't say you'd *be* happy, just that you'll tend to become happy. Becoming a Buddha is like this. Act as if you were already Buddha, and it will tend to make you Buddha. That's the whole premise of this book, and indeed of spiritual practice in general, everywhere, always.

Acting as if you were Buddha makes you an image of the Buddha, not the real thing. But don't diss yourself: you are not imitating the Buddha; you are practicing Buddha behavior. Be who you really are—someone who's trying. This is authentically you, even though the exterior behavior may feel forced. Remember, to be someone who's trying to be Buddha is a tremendous aspiration and the beginning of tremendous achievement.

What I've just said is not only the basis of the Buddha's path to happiness, it's also the basis of Buddhist ethics—and not only

Buddhist ethics, but Aristotelian ethics as well. Both the Buddha and Aristotle were seeking the path to happiness. For both of them, deep happiness was the goal of life. And both of them knew the path had to be discovered and traveled over time. So there. This book is not just a bag of tricks. It's the fundamental basis of all morality and happiness, East and West. Ha! When you practice even shallowly, you begin to acquire a habit. That is excellent—literally. You acquire the virtuous excellence of a habit that leads you and the world, ever so slowly, to the good. That's what this book is all about.

What You'll Find Here

I've divided this book into six chapters full of scenarios and solutions covering various aspects of life. These are real situations every one of us faces, with real solutions you can achieve. The separate chapters make it easy for folks with specific problems to skip right to specific solutions when they need them. But you'll probably want to read through the book at leisure. As you go through the chapters (which you don't have to do in order), you'll see how each scenario I describe illuminates a common annoyance in life, and each Buddhist solution I offer shows you how to transcend that annoyance.

As you become familiar with the book, you'll notice that the scenarios in each chapter have commonalities with each other. So do the solutions. By the end of each chapter, you'll begin to understand how all the chapter's solutions come together into a coherent technique for enriching that aspect of life. By the end of the book, you'll begin to see how all the practices in the chapters come together to give you not only a positive outlook on life but a varied set of practices to make your life more positive.

This book describes 72 problems and gives 72 (actually, a few more) solutions to those problems. Some will click for you right away.

Some will take some time to work. Some may even irritate or bore you. No problem, 72 is a lot of solutions. If even just a few become parts of your life, this book will have done its job. And if it leads you on to deeper practices, so much the better, but that's not its job. Its job is to make you happier, right now, right where you are.

Using What You Find

You'll recognize the scenarios, and you'll easily understand the quick solutions I offer for them. It's all very "real-world." You don't have to worry about following complex and difficult instructions or finding obscure and expensive paraphernalia.

In fact, this is such seemingly simple stuff that you might not immediately recognize the solutions as Buddhist. Don't worry about it. When they're connected to vital aspects of Buddhism, I'll explain how, but it may not matter to you. What matters is just doing the practices. I'm not giving them to you as a religion. I'm giving them to you as practical tricks to make you happier. That was the Buddha's bottom line, and it's my bottom line as well. His Holiness the Dalai Lama tells us that the purpose of life is to be happy; all living things want to be happy. No argument here.

So, I don't care if you're Buddhist or Baptist or Baha'i—just be happy. Really, there's no need to convert or even to learn much about Buddhism. I personally think learning about Buddhism is wonderful, and I've spent my whole adult life doing it. There are profound things to discover in exploring the Four Noble Truths, the Eightfold Path, the Five Precepts, the Ten Perfections, and all the practices, teachings, and persons that make up the 2500 years of the Buddha-sasana. But such exploration is not crucial on the path to awakening, let alone to happiness. And being a Buddhist certainly is not crucial either.

What is a "Buddhist" after all? Is it someone who has taken refuge in the Buddha, the *dharma* (Buddhist teaching), and the *sangha* (Buddhist community)? If you want answers to questions like "Who's a Buddhist?" "Who was Buddha?" or "What is Buddhism?" then go straight to the appendix for further sources. Everything between here and the appendix is about things you can do.

What is crucial, then? What do we absolutely have to do to be happier? We have to learn who we are (and aren't) and how we fit into this world. When we learn that, the rest will fall into place. Ah, but learning can be hard. I spent 28 years in school—28 years!—so I got pretty good at learning. Yet even an overeducated person like me can learn better by doing than by studying. So this book teaches you how to do simple, practical things that can change your life. The Buddha himself said we should try his path, and he knew that "try" means both "sample" and "put on trial." We should walk the path and see where it gets us. For the Buddha and me, experiencing the path is what matters. If you're becoming happier through living with more wisdom and compassion, who cares if you don't fully know what you're doing?

I won't lie to you; some of the practices in this book are tough, no question about it. Sometimes working is tough. Sometimes loving is tough. Sometimes staying healthy is tough. Sometimes parenting is tough. And, of course, sometimes finding meaning and spiritual peace is tough, and that's what we're doing here. Still, what I show you in this book is not arcane, egg-headed, or woo-woo. It makes sense in a way that you can feel the rightness of. You don't need a Ph.D. to understand it. You can feel its rightness because it grows directly from the Buddha's teachings and responds directly to our lives. It makes sense because it works.

The Buddha's First Teaching

Is it a surprise so many Buddhist solutions grow from opening one-self to reality? It shouldn't be; this fundamental movement has been the central, unifying goal of Buddhism from the time the Buddha began teaching. That makes the rest of Buddhism the means to that end, to that opening. The end is always the same for everyone (at least as much as reality is the same for everyone—which I admit is an assertion that's open to debate).

Conversely, the means are exquisitely differentiated throughout space and time. In other words, the means are really different for everyone.

The central means of Buddhism are explained in the first teaching the Buddha gave just after his awakening when he spoke of finding "the middle path," or "the middle way." He had tried paths of self-indulgence and self-denial and found that they only led to *dukkha*, or worldly pain and suffering. Once he changed course and began following a middle path, he awakened to reality By avoiding these two extremes, the Buddha has gained knowledge of the middle path which gives insight and wisdom, and leads to calm, to vision, to awakening, to nirvana.

> *O monks, what is the middle path, which gives insight and knowledge, and leads to calm, to vision, to awakening, to nirvana? It is the noble eightfold path: right view, right intention, right speech, right action, right livelihood, right effort, right mindfulness, right concentration.*

Samyutta Nikaya LVI.11,
the *Dhammacakkapavattana Sutta*
(First Turning of the Wheel of Truth)

Those few words pretty well lay it out: the means (following the Eightfold Path) and the end (calm, vision, awakening, nirvana). Throughout the rest of his life, perhaps 45 more years, the Buddha carefully developed what the path entailed. After his death his students continued developing it, and then their students, and the great monks of ancient days, and the inspired authors of the Mahayana sutras, and the brilliant teachers of the many Buddhist schools, and the pioneering priests who brought Buddhism across the seas, and their creative successors who have transmitted the teachings to us, and even contemporary writers who bring you little books like this one. We are all working on the means to the end. We are all widening the path, smoothing it, improving the signage as we can.

This entire book is a collection of my own ways of bringing the eightfold path to life—my life. For example, the Buddha says follow right speech; I'll give you the trick I use to shut myself up when I'm yelling at my wife. It's the same thing. Or, rather, my trick is one little part of the Buddha's great technique of right speech. It's one variation among the thousands or millions of tricks Buddhists have made up and taught and learned over the last 2500 years, as we've tried to follow right speech, walking the Eightfold Path. Each of my solutions in this book is an effort to stay on the path or get back on the path when I've lost it. Each expands on one or more aspects of the Eightfold Path, whether I mention it or not. You don't have to know you're following the path. You just have to keep going. You're on your way to calm, to vision, to awakening, to nirvana.

This book puts you on the path. I once wrote that the path is before us all at once. The path invites practice all the time. The path has no beginning. The path does not end. I add now one of the Four Great Vows: "Dharma gates are endless. I vow to enter them." They are endless because they are open to us at every moment, in every situation. We vow to enter them because that is life.

Try it.

A new monk came to Teacher Xuansha and asked where he could enter the truth of the teachings. Xuansha asked, "Do you hear the sound of the local stream?" The monk said yes. Xuansha said, "Enter there."

1

Out in the World

WELCOME TO THE WORLD!
Well, okay, it's not always the nicest place, and you don't always feel
welcome here. Siddhartha Gautama felt just the same way. That's
why he went into the forest to meditate for five years: to try to get
to the bottom of why he felt so ill at ease in the world, to try to find
a cure for his pain. The cure Siddhartha found made him the Buddha,
which literally means "The Awakened." He returned to the world
fully at ease with his role as a human being and as a teacher.

In the earliest Buddhist scriptures, the Buddha is called by many
names, including Dispeller of Darkness, Teacher of Divine and Human Beings, Unsurpassed Doctor and Surgeon, Wielder of Power,
and, one of my personal favorites, Bull among Men. Usually he's
called Blessed One or Lord, not because of any kind of divine nature, but because of what he achieved and shared with us. Among
the many names the Buddha is called and calls himself is "Expert
on the World."

This is good. If the Buddha is an expert on the world—the ultimate self-help guru, combining the best of Deepak Chopra, Dr. Phil, and Jesus—then he can help us not only with the subtleties of meditation or the details of living the monastic life; he can help us with the world, at work, in our relationships, with our bodies and house paints and car payments and mothers-in-law. Now that's what I call an Expert on the World! That's a spiritual leader I can learn from right here, right now.

We usually think of the Buddha quite differently: as a contemplative ascetic meditating in solitude. But the Buddha spent only five years in the forest. For the first 25 years he was a prince, living in the center of power and intrigue in his kingdom. And after that five-year interlude, he spent the next 45 years or so traveling, often to big cities, and teaching, often to the heavy hitters of his time. The Buddha was a guy with real savvy. Not just good looks and a feel-good spiel, but a genuine appreciation of the way the world works and, especially, the way human minds work.

We can use clues from the Buddha to make our own worlds and our own minds better places to live in—real nuts-and-bolt stuff. This whole book is packed with things you can do; but let's start off with a contrast, a palate-cleanser, something you can't do.

When You Should *Not* Say the Nembutsu

I and the world know that you're cheating and lying. I can tell you're stealing HBO. I see you eating fruit in the supermarket. Little things add up. Next thing you know, you're selling your company stock for enormous sums while you rip off billions of dollars and drive your corporation into the ground, destroying the lives of thousands of employees. You know this is bad. You feel guilty and want forgiveness from God or the Buddha or somebody.

Here's the rule: do not—repeat, *do not*—make some lame offering to the Buddha, thinking it will make up for your faults and everything will be okay. These days, people in public life seem to think that as long as they apologize, they've balanced the scales and undone the harm. When you intentionally create harm, you have to change, not apologize. Apologizing is only the beginning. Even then, you shouldn't be apologizing to the Buddha, you should apologize to the people who have been hurt by your actions.

Nor can you make up for harmful actions with gifts or prayers. One way people have traditionally tried to make amends is by saying the *nembutsu*—the phrase "*Namu Amida Butsu*" ("Praise Amida Buddha").

> Followers of Pure Land Buddhism, perhaps the most popular form of Buddhism in the world, believe that long ago a *bodhisattva*, or "awakened being," made a vow to save all sentient beings by bringing them to the Pure Land, a place where everybody will have the strength and leisure to reach nirvana. That bodhisattva vowed not to become a full Buddha until this had happened. But because he has become the great celestial Buddha called Amida, Pure Land Buddhists believe his vow must have been fulfilled and Amida is surely able to help us suffering beings reach the Pure Land after this life—or maybe even during it. In fact, if Amida is a Buddha, then Amida has *already* helped them reach the Pure Land. So, repeating the name Amida Buddha in hope and gratitude has become the central practice of the hundreds of millions of Pure Land Buddhists around the world.

Saying the nembutsu is a great practice, and there are definitely times to say it when you've caused harm unintentionally. But if you've done intentional harm, Don't call on Amida to help you out of the mess you've caused. You are going to have to deal with it yourself.

Now that I've told you what not to do, here's something you can do. Instead of "Namu Amida Buddha," say "I can change." You may remain pretty weak, but you'll be stronger than before. As you get stronger, you'll change. And as you change, you will make things right again.

So much for what not to do. I'm saying that words do not make up for actions. I'm also saying we need to look forward, not back. We need to accept our situations and respond to them actively. When we do this, our situations, even annoying ones, can become opportunities.

Telling ourselves we can change is our first positive response. It's true; we can change, and coming to believe that is vital to making great progress in life. Yet before we can believe that, we need to hear it. So telling ourselves we can change comes before the deeper changes occur. Telling leads to believing, and believing leads to doing.

Good. Now for a simple and frustratingly common scene where we can starting doing.

Traffic Grinds to a Total Halt

You are on the way to work, school, an appointment, or anyplace else where you need to arrive on time. You've allowed a full 13 minutes for your 17 minute ride. Oops. Then there's parking to contend with. You know you'll have to make up for lost time once you're there, even though you already have umpteen things on your plate for the rest of the day. As you're worrying about all this, the traffic loses its passionate intensity and, seeming to lack all conviction, stops.

Being trapped in traffic is a remarkable situation. If you're like me, you are almost certainly ready to get pissed off as soon as traffic stops. But consider the actual situation. You're comfortable, quiet, and alone. Although you're surrounded by other people, they're minding their own business and are not going to bother you unless you let them. You have full control over your internal world. You are a monk in your own little meditation cell. You know how you always wish you had just a few minutes to calm down and think about things? These are your minutes. Use them!

Plan your presentation strategy. Do a breathing exercise. Think of a few things you want to say in a letter to an old friend—or just call him. There are plenty of things you can do with this precious time. Start with a simple breath exercise. Breath in, feel the expansion in your lungs. Breath out, feel the relaxing of your muscles. Turn the vexation into a blessing.

You may not feel that a traffic jam is the ideal time and place for it, but you've been given the gift of a solo retreat. A colleague of mine, Rachel Harris, has even written a whole book called *20-Minute Retreats*. That's the extraordinary thing about the spiritual dimension of our lives: it's always available, right now, whatever we're doing. We just have to wake up to it.

With the opening provided by the simplest breath meditation—nothing scary, really just a relaxation—we can turn our trapped selves in trapped cars into free beings with free time. Remember dharma gates are endlessly opening. This is a perfect example. The traffic jam is a dharma gate. When you enter it, where does it take you? You're free to go there. When you string enough of them together for a long enough time, openings such as this look a whole lot like what the Buddha taught.

> The monk Nagarjuna, considered by many the greatest philosopher of Mahayana Buddhism, wrote "There is no distinction whatsoever between samsara and nirvana, and there is no distinction between nirvana and samsara. The limit of nirvana and the limit of samsara: one cannot find even the slightest difference between them" (*Mulamadhyamakakarika* 19-20).
>
> The good news is, this messed up, dreary, painful, fleeting world of samsara is really the perfect, blissful, eternal world of nirvana. Excellent! The bad news is, the perfect world of nirvana is really this messed up world of samsara. Bummer. I (and now you) have Professor Richard Hayes to thank for this observation. What Dr. Hayes and Nagarjuna are offering us is immediate liberation. If samsara and nirvana are the same thing, then all it takes to leave one and enter the other is a shift in mind. to enter nirvana we

merely need to shift into experiencing the world as nirvana. Nothing to it. Okay, you first. . . .

Right, since we're ready to start stringing dharma gate openings together, here's another you'll experience any day now.

In Line at the Post Office

There you are at the post office. No, wait; that's not bad enough. You're at the DMV. I'm sorry, but it happens and now it's happened to you. There you are amid the spectacle of a thousand other people who loathe being there, even the ones getting paid for it. Maybe especially them. Imagine that job. Oh, and it's hot. Too hot. You are bored, and your boredom is slowly turning to frustration and anger. The line hasn't moved for ten minutes! What is wrong with these people?!

Okay, maybe that's too much. The DMV is profound practice; maybe I'll write about that in another 20 years. The post office is bad enough to offer a good fundamental practice place. Amazing how it can take people five whole minutes to negotiate the intricacies of buying a stamp. So, there you are, watching it unfold. Time slows down to the glacial pace of the line. What can you do?

It is exceptionally difficult to think straight in a post office. I somehow never manage to do anything that moves my career forward while I'm there. It's not the postal service's fault, it's mine— but I have a back-up plan. I just check out the people in line with me, and this is my advice for you, too. Really *look* at the sentient beings in line with you. In Hollywood, where I live, the folks in the post office line are fascinating. There's nary a film star among them. Perhaps celebrities have their own secret post offices somewhere. No, people in my line are just folks—all races and religions, old and young, bored or pissed off. They wear funky clothes, and their kids run around like barnyard animals. When I really look at them, they're enthralling. The trick here is to leap out of your self-concern and just look. Then you let go of yourself standing in line (which is absolutely boring) and open yourself to experiencing the other, vibrantly strange people.

 I view "just looking" as a variation on Zen teacher Dogen's "just sitting." In a way it's harder because of the distractions in the post office. But in a way it's also easier because of them. Such distractions really help break you out of your circular, self-concerned thinking. This allows experiencing others for who they are, and it can lead to a real increase in compassion. That, in turn, breaks down the barriers we are constantly erecting between others and us. It all begins with just standing there and really seeing people. Next thing you know, the clerk is calling you to the window.

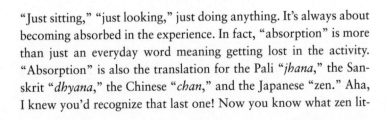

"Just sitting," "just looking," just doing anything. It's always about becoming absorbed in the experience. In fact, "absorption" is more than just an everyday word meaning getting lost in the activity. "Absorption" is also the translation for the Pali "*jhana,*" the Sanskrit "*dhyana,*" the Chinese "*chan,*" and the Japanese "*zen.*" Aha, I knew you'd recognize that last one! Now you know what zen literally means. It means absorption, particularly absorption in meditation. That's why I say "just looking" is something like Zen's "just sitting." But all life can be like this. The most impressive people I've ever met, people who have really awakened themselves, are Zen teachers. They're so impressive because they embody this absorption so much of the time. They have such presence because they're so present themselves.

Being present to each moment as we experience (and create) our worlds is vital. Yet simply being present is not always enough to get things done and keep up with the pace of the day. We need further solutions to further problems we face. So let's turn our attention from being in the moment to planning ahead for future moments. The Buddha never said the past and future don't matter. On the contrary, as the exiled Vietnamese monk Thich Nhat Hanh teaches, the future will be made only of the present, an endless string of future presents, beginning with this one. We need to take care of the present in relation to that future.

That's all very heady. So here's a very un-heady illustration.

One Way to Stop Yourself from Running Late

We all run late. It's an epidemic, and since we all do it ourselves, we cut others slack when they do it as well. But, fundamentally, running late is a statement about your relationship with other people. If you habitually run late, you are saying "I'm more important than you. Your inconvenience is not enough to make me alter my day."

This is one of my own persistent faults. I struggle to be on time because I plan the steps of my day as best-case scenarios. The trouble is, my day doesn't work out that way. The shirt I was going to wear needs ironing, someone calls just as I'm leaving, the traffic is bad, and on and on. These things are not our fault; we're off the hook, or so we think. But believing they won't happen to us is our fault. We're back on it again.

Here's what to do to combat lateness and to center yourself: leave twice as much time for driving as you think it could possibly take. This way you get three likely scenarios, all of them excellent:

1) You arrive early and have time to say hello, check out the space, go to the bathroom, window shop—in short, enjoy a little spare time for a change.

2) You leave later than you want but still arrive on time. You are empowered by how together you feel when you arrive.

3) You hit traffic, but, since you left so early, you are able to use traffic time for calming yourself, maybe doing a breath meditation, thinking about your projects, or dreaming of a better world. Everyone else arrives frazzled; you arrive mindful and centered.

Buddhist progress comes through several kinds of practice. One central practice is replacing harmful behaviors with helpful behaviors. Sounds "everyday," not "spiritual," doesn't it? Darn right. Just what would be the problem with that? Fundamental practice is all about, well, practicing the fundamentals. Replace your harmful habit of leaving late with a helpful habit of leaving early. This requires effort—but it's practical effort.

Okay, it's also spiritual effort. Leaving earlier than you think necessary allows time for the instant of opening that breaks us out into becoming the Buddha. This is our continual challenge and we need to give ourselves every chance for it. It just takes an instant. Give yourself that instant.

Now we're really seeing how "fundamental" fundamental practice is. We're also seeing how "practical" fundamental practice is. Here's another practice you might not have thought of as spiritual.

Why Recycling Is Bodhisattva Practice

I know, recycling is a pain in the butt. I'm lucky, in L.A. they let us throw all recyclables together in one bin. But my parents in San Francisco have to sort everything. My dad has had to write detailed instructions on the tops of all these different tubs around the kitchen. I'm sorely tempted to just trash stuff when I visit, but I don't even know which bin is the trash! Recycling *is* a pain outside, too, when there are no recycling bins. I mean, do you really want to carry that plastic water bottle all the way home? Of course you do. Well, okay, you don't, but here's a way to encourage yourself to want to.

Think of that plastic bottle as an offering to the *sangha*. All over Asia (and now in the West) Buddhists make offerings to the sangha, the community of monks and nuns. The larger sangha is all Buddhists, even all people, and in fact all living things. When you take that bottle home and recycle it, you are offering it to the environment, the sangha of all living things. What a noble act that is! Don't deprive yourself of that opportunity. Keep the bottle in your purse or briefcase. If it could fit there when it was full, it can certainly fit there empty. It's valuable. Take it home, and when you do finally arrive at your recycling bin, maybe make a little bow as you give your offering. And remember, you're a living thing, too. You deserve a bow for this gift.

Of course, the toughest part may be for you to make it home to recycle. When you're tempted to throw that bottle away—and, even more, when you're tempted to litter or dump your engine oil or something similarly loathsome—visualize throwing that bottle right in the Buddha's face. Right in the kisser. You don't want to do that, right? This image will help you hold onto that bottle.

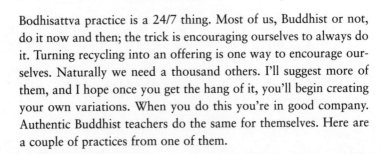

Bodhisattva practice is a 24/7 thing. Most of us, Buddhist or not, do it now and then; the trick is encouraging ourselves to always do it. Turning recycling into an offering is one way to encourage ourselves. Naturally we need a thousand others. I'll suggest more of them, and I hope once you get the hang of it, you'll begin creating your own variations. When you do this you're in good company. Authentic Buddhist teachers do the same for themselves. Here are a couple of practices from one of them.

Road Hazards

I don't mean ice or dips or gravel. I mean the most dangerous hazards of all: people. We get intensely frustrated when other drivers we're sharing the road with don't measure up. What's fascinating to me is that it happens whether or not the wrong conduct of other drivers affects my drive. Picture yourself on the freeway, going the speed limit, when some lunatic comes up from behind, doing 85mph, weaving like a NASCAR driver (without the professional skills) dropped into the middle of your commute. I don't know about you, but this really bugs me. Let's be clear: this fool is not slowing me down, but he bugs me all the same. It's not about him effecting my trip, it's about him affecting my mind.

The situation is even worse when another driver does affect my drive. Say, when instead of going 85 mph, he's going 45 mph . . . in the fast lane. These people drive me insane (briefly insane, but insane nevertheless). Luckily, I've benefited from two practices from Zen teacher Taigen Dan Leighton Sensei. Here's what he does.

When the rabid racer whizzes by, don't think he's an idiot, instead think he's just learned a loved one is in the emergency room. He's got to get there as quickly as possible. Of course you don't know if this is true, but it doesn't matter. If you can believe it, it immediately relieves your anger. You can even add a prayer for the person in the ER, if you like.

As for the lame driver blocking your way, just take a breath and think "This person is a bodhisattva; he's protecting me from driving too fast; he's making me aware of my own impatience;

he's my teacher." Naturally, the other half of this practice is to stop tailgating the slow driver and just pass naturally, thankful for the moment.

Driving, like all things, is not about the destination, it's about the journey. And so it's not about you, or getting there first. It's about the whole stream of traffic traveling there together.

Leighton Sensei really is a bodhisattva and an authorized Zen teacher, so his "Zen driver's ed" is, in a sense, a traditional Buddhist practice. You won't find it in any books, though, except this one.

Now let's turn to an entirely different arena of practice, one that just might seem more "spiritual."

When It's Time to Re-up for Another Year of Charity

If you're like me, you don't keep very good track of your charitable contributions. People come by the door and you can't say no. Or you get those envelopes covered with heart-wrenching pictures of doe-eyed children or childlike does. You succumb. Good for you. Then another year slides by, and you get another envelope reminding you it's time to re-up. Hey, if you gave once, why not give again? It's not that these organizations are slacking off or that the creatures with such soft eyes last year have suddenly become Microsoft executives. And yet, admit it, you feel conflict. You can't give to everyone, but everyone asks. Giving has lost its ease.

Here's one way to clarify your feelings. *Jataka* 390, a tale of a prior life of the Buddha, teaches "Charity is fruitful only when we feel the three pure feelings: feeling joy before the gift is given, giving gracefully, and having pleasure of it after; that is perfect charity."

Apply this teaching to your life. It just takes a moment. When that donation request comes in, breathe comfortably and open the letter. Don't analyze it; let your emotions happen. Ask yourself three questions. Did I feel good upon seeing the letter, looking forward to giving? Am I relaxed and comfortable right now, as I'm considering the act of giving? And, looking back on last year, am I happy about having given? If you're comfortable and happy, then give. If not, then don't. Give only if you feel good about it. There are a thousand other worthy causes. Your power lies not only in giving, it lies in choosing whom to give to.

There you have it: a simple solution to the problem of giving, and permission to feel good about your giving. We all need our props. I like that term because it seems to offer support in two ways: something to lean on and also kudos for our practice.

Here's another prop that often leads to its own reward. . . .

How to Stop Yourself from Gossiping

A couple of friends have been having relationship problems. You spot one of them at a concert with another partner. You can just sense this is no platonic thing and you come home dying to tell mutual friends about it. Danger!

Gossip can be delicious fun to spread, but it deeply undermines work situations, families, schools, you name it. It nearly always gets back to the people involved, and when that happens, it ruins trust. In fact, it ruins trust even before, because if you know you're gossiping, you can be sure others are gossiping about you. You've got to stop this process.

Gossip is one form of "wrong speech"; Right Speech is part of the Eightfold Path, so if you start in with wrong speech and you've abandoned the path. Uh-oh, that sounds bad. How bad? Well, the Eightfold Path is Buddhism itself. It's the way to walk the path of the Buddha in your own life. According to the Buddhist canons, the various collections of Buddhist scriptures, the Eightfold Path was taught in the very first sermon the Buddha ever gave. He talked about dukkha and nirvana and said the way to go from one to the other was to follow the Eightfold Path.

For the record, the Eightfold Path is: Right View, Right Intention, Right Speech, Right Action, Right Livelihood, Right Effort, Right Mindfulness, and Right Concentration. The eight factors are traditionally lumped into three groups. The first two are about wisdom, that is, understanding the way the world is. The next three are about morality, living life with compassion for all beings. The last three are about meditation, cultivating increasing insight and absorption in our minds.

So, yes, Buddhism teaches that it's really bad to gossip.

Back to the scenario: you've seen the potential affair. Now let's say you're with a friend who knows all these people and is going to relish hearing your suspicions. You're just about to blab. Who knows what pain that could lead to down the line? Here's how to stop before you say too much:

> Quickly pretend you're not talking to your friend, but to the Buddha. Instead of blabbing, say something or ask something worthy of your time with the Awakened One. Make it good; the Buddha is a busy guy. Not only will this prevent you from gossiping, it sets you up for a really worthwhile talk with your buddy.

In my experience, Right Speech and Right Concentration are the most difficult aspects of the path, so this practice helps me where I need it. For some other people, Right Livelihood is the toughest part of the Eightfold Path. Right Livelihood requires having a job that helps the world and then doing good work at that job. That's a tall order. If you have a dull job, a tedious job, a normal job, there are many practices you can do at work to help things along. With BJ Gallagher I wrote a whole book on bringing Buddhism to your livelihood, *What Would Buddha Do at Work?*, so there's help available. Here's a trio of quick solutions to common problems we all face at work, some of us every day.

Ending Boredom at Work

Work varies. Sometimes it's so demanding you can't keep up. This is difficult, of course, but at least it's engrossing and passes the time. Sometimes, though, work is so tedious you can actually fall asleep on the job with embarrassing and sometimes dangerous results. Gotta snap out of it.

When you're totally bored at work, try this: pretend it's your last day on the job. Take this seriously. On your last day, you plainly can't finish anything long-term, but you can do little things you've always intended to do but never got around to. Tackle one or another of those things. This is your moment to thank that person for just being cool, or to clean up the shelves by the water cooler, or to put up some cartoons for the next guy. Anything that springs to mind. Start by imagining that it's your last day, and your creative mind will give you plenty of ideas for stuff to do.

One note of caution: Do not tell off your boss! Remember, this is fantasy, not reality. You don't want to *really* make this your last day!

Speaking of bosses. . . .

Being Your Boss's Mother

There are tough bosses; there are mean bosses; and there are downright evil bosses. They probably don't have weapons of mass destruction—they aren't *that* evil—but if they're taking pleasure in intentionally harming you and other workers, they are doing evil. Fortunately, I've never had a boss like that, though I did have a teacher or two like that during my long years in school. I didn't know any way to deal with them but anger and resentment. Now I do, and I want to arm you with it.

Let's say you're a carpenter, and your boss tells you to build him a house. So you do, and when it's done he says "I hate it. Build another." Then he tears it down. So you build another, and he tears that one down too. And another, and again he destroys it. Of course you will come to hate this boss because of the way he delights in making you suffer needlessly. He's wasting both your time and his resources. It's insane, but he keeps it up. You may be tempted to some kind of revenge, blatant or anonymous. But if you succumb to this impulse, he will take the frustration it causes him out on you, even if he doesn't know you did it. As any wise Buddhist teacher would tell you, this is not the great and noble way. You have to trust that karma, the universal law of cause and effect, is inescapable. Your boss may appear to be successful, but do you think this creep is happy? Do you think he has real friends or real love? No, his own harmful actions surround him with harmful consequences. That's how karma works.

 Since you can't take revenge, here's what you can do to ease your own feelings of victimization. See your boss as your child. Imagine you're his mother. You love him, and it pains you to see him so angry and mean. When you experience his venting (even at you), look at it as the childish tantrum of a toddler. You can't truly stay angry at toddlers; they're too puny and helpless. They lack awareness of their failings. So thinking of your boss as your foolish child gives you a place for patience and even compassion for actions you could not otherwise tolerate.

This does not mean you need to passively stay in this terrible job. If your boss has only partial power over you, you have recourse to reviews, lateral promotions, etc. And even if he does have total control over you in the workplace, he doesn't have control over his superiors and teammates. Make sure they know your work. Get their letters of recommendation. Think ahead; you are not alone.

By the way, the illustration of a boss who tears down the houses you build comes from the ancient story of Marpa and Milarepa. Milarepa was a young sorcerer who practiced black magic but wanted to learn Buddhism. As a first step in his studies, his teacher, Marpa, had him build a house, but whenever Milarepa finished it, Marpa would have him tear it down and start again. This drove Milarepa crazy, but he kept on working. In the end he began to learn about discipline, about humility, and about the mercy of his teacher who was helping him burn off his very bad karma. So don't take revenge on your boss. You never know who he might really be.

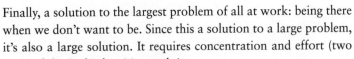

Finally, a solution to the largest problem of all at work: being there when we don't want to be. Since this a solution to a large problem, it's also a large solution. It requires concentration and effort (two parts of the Path), but it's worth it.

Why Do You Do This Damn Job, Anyway?

Work can get pretty dull and unrewarding. There are many reasons for this. Some are large and theoretical. Marx's well-proven concept of "alienated labor"—the loss of the worker's direct connection to work and direct reward for the products they create—is one of them. Such alienation can be frustrating and unfair.

> Yes, this tidbit of Marxism is observably true. Even though Marx has lost his credibility lately—and for good reason—he was still a smart guy with powerful ideas, and this is one of his greatest insights about modern life.

There are other reasons for work being dull. Perhaps your reason is the boredom of repeating the same paperwork or motions over and over. Perhaps it's the frustration of making one more cold sales call or straightening out one more confused inventory. Such drains on our energy distance us from the reasons we go to work in the first place.

When you experience such a drain and forget why you took this stupid job in the first place, you probably have good reason for feeling that way. Yet you can't let yourself get stuck in that place; it is poison to you. Once again, you need to change your mind. It helps to remind yourself exactly why it is that you go to work.

 Ask yourself, "Why am I here?" and see what comes up. Ask it repeatedly and keep working on refining your answers. When you've got at least a tentative answer, put it to work. Make a short phrase from it, short enough to remember and repeat. Since I'm lucky enough to enjoy my work (well, most of the time), one of my answers is "I write to spread insight." Another is "I teach to deepen my students' lives." Perhaps you, too, have found Right Livelihood and can formulate something similar. But perhaps the reason you work is just to make money. That's good, too. Why do you make money? To support your family? Then say "I'm here because I love my kids." There are as many reasons as there are people. Find the reasons that are your own.

You can repeat your phrase several times a day, whenever you need it most, like when the alarm goes off in the morning, or perhaps when walking out to the car or sitting down at your desk. You can also repeat your intention as a kind of reward, reminding yourself of what you've accomplished. In this case you can say it just as you leave work, maybe as you turn your computer off or change out of your work clothes. Say it when you truly feel your day is done. Why did you work today? Remind yourself and give yourself credit.

I started off this chapter by writing about when you shouldn't say the nembutsu. It's about time to write about when you should. Here is one specific example. You'll think of others.

When to Say the Nembutsu

You're driving on a country road and see the remains of an animal that has been run over. You might not even know what kind of animal it was, but you can tell it was alive, it wanted to live, and now it's dead. You are sad. Or you may be driving on a country road and see an animal right in front of your headlights—an instant before you run it over. How horrible this is! I still so vividly remember the look of shock and confusion in the eyes of a possum as I hit it, many years ago. That poor thing, if there were only something I could do for it!

Well, perhaps there is. When you feel sorrow for another living thing, offer your feelings of sorrow and well-wishing to it in the form of the nembutsu: saying "Namu Amida Butsu." Yes, exactly the phrase I told you earlier not to say. This situation is completely different. Before, I was describing the unworthy urge to make up for intentional harm as cheaply as possible. Now I'm talking about the worthy urge to make better a broken world. This deeply compassionate feeling is something to treasure. As you say "Namu Amida Butsu. Namu Amida Butsu. Namu Amida Butsu," you bless the broken world and praise the Buddha who helps you feel and share these blessings!

Don't limit yourself. I say this whenever I accidentally kill anything, and often when I see something that's been killed. But you can also say it when you've thought a harmful thought, or shot a mean look at someone you love. If you didn't really mean these things and you sincerely feel bad about them, say the nembutsu and you'll empower your own compassion. You can also say it when you feel what the Japanese call *mono no aware*, a sense of the unending melancholy of the world. It can be your gift to the cosmos. Come up with your own times to say it. How about right now?

The beauty of saying the nembutsu is that whether it works for the other being or not, you know it works for you. It makes you increasingly aware of your compassion and your power to strengthen and harness that compassion. It's a perfect example of how practice makes perfect.

This broken world always needs our help. We help it by strengthening our wisdom and compassion, and we help it by translating those virtues into action. Even the smallest actions add up.

Why Cleanliness Is Next to Godliness

Have you ever really thought about that old saw "Cleanliness is next to godliness"? I never understood it until I read Gary Thorp's book on the spirituality of cleaning, *Sweeping Changes*. In it he shows us how to use the need for cleaning our homes as a constant opportunity for Buddhist practice. Taking a cue from Thorp, here's a way to practice and maybe get closer to godliness.

Imagine yourself cleaning something pretty nasty, say the toilet. Cleaning such a thing gives us a chance to face reality in a way we usually recoil from. The fact is, we are bodies, and we constantly produce all sorts of effluvia we think of as nasty. We're nonstop mess machines. So there you are with your face right up against the reality of piss and shit. How can you transform this potentially nauseating experience into a potentially liberating one?

To do this you need to actually have the experience and unwrap it from its evaluative container. Notice what's happening in your mind and, with part of your attention, give it a name. For instance, let yourself see, the yellow spots and the brown residues. Do you feel grossed out? Then let yourself be grossed out, and at the same time label it as "feeling grossed out." Don't evaluate the experience or hold onto it; keep turning your awareness to the job at hand: cleaning. Whether your experience is "nausea" or "knees hurting" or "cold hands" or "impatience," just feel it, label it, and let yourself move on to the next experience.

None of these experiences is intrinsically bad. We make them bad by thinking they should be bad, trapping ourselves in a situation that is, by definition, bad. Thinking you are suffering, holding your breath and averting your eyes, only makes things worse. It creates an experience of "Ugh, horrible, must get away but can't!" instead of "Hmmm, unpleasant, better clean this quick and make things better."

Cleaning places and things other than bathrooms is easier. Instead of being grossed out, you may only be bored. Again, let yourself experience the cleaning rather than your aversion to it. An aversion to cleaning has no up side since you can't stop cleaning. If you did, you'd be lost in filth. Cleaning is an endless battle that can never be won, but from which there is no retreat. All important things are like this. Love, work, and life itself are like this: we always lose them in the end. Experience the now without judgment.

The method of cleaning I just described is really a variation on mindfulness meditation. When you're cleaning like that—really open to

the experience, unwrapping it and just letting it happen—you are, in effect, meditating. Naturally, there are deeper methods of cultivating sati, or mindfulness, and many meditative techniques designed to increase it. The Buddha teaches *anapanasati* (mindfulness of breath) meditation in the scriptures. You can find instructions online and in books and hear them from many teachers. Such meditation instructions don't belong here, but I hope you can see how these most fundamental practices open out endlessly onto the realm of awakening. For tips on finding online meditation instructions, check out the resources in "Just Add More" at the end of this book.

Here is another practice that opens out into real depth, like the cleaning practice does:

The Fellowship of the Ringing

I don't know about you, but I have a love-hate relationship with my phone. I love to talk on the phone, but I also love space and silence, so I hate being interrupted by the ringing of the phone. Imagine you're reading that novel you finally found time to get around to. You're settled down in your favorite reading chair, maybe you've got your tea all made and you're warm and snuggly . . . and the phone rings. Maybe it's all the way over in the kitchen, two rooms away across the cold floor. Arrrgh! Or perhaps you're having a beautiful moment with your partner, in which you're once again reminded how blessed you are to be with such a person who brings out the love you never felt so . . . riiiiiinnnnnggggg. Now *that* is annoying. And don't even get me started on what it's like when that ring was initiated by a telemarketer or a machine. Grrrrr.

Here's a practice I try to do in these situations. Dan Taigen Leighton taught it to me, and he, in turn, got it from working at Parallax Press, a Buddhist publisher; now I am offering it to you. (See how good karma can expand?)

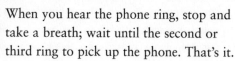 When you hear the phone ring, stop and take a breath; wait until the second or third ring to pick up the phone. That's it. Very easy, but when you wait, you give yourself a chance to let your tension, anger, or worry subside. You allow your mind to empty and be receptive to the needs of the person on the other end. This emptying is an opening to wisdom and compassion.

If that's easy for you, you can add another element. Think of the call as a chance to send *metta*, which means "friendship." On the phone you can send friendly wishes out beyond your self. As you let it ring a few times, think to yourself, "Whoever is calling was my mother in a previous lifetime. I will show her my gratitude."

Nice little trick, and, who knows, it might be true. Let it inspire you.

As the cleaning trick opens onto mindfulness meditation, the ringing trick opens onto metta meditation. Both are traditional and central forms of Buddhist practice. I called metta "friendship," but it's usually translated as "loving-kindness." I think that's because it also opens onto a depth that mere friendship doesn't seem to contain. When we practice metta meditation, we send good wishes to loved ones, to neutral people, and even to enemies. Perhaps we can't send friendship to enemies, but we can send loving-kindness. We can love their essential humanity and be kind to them, hoping to help them change.

Let's conclude this chapter with a big thought. We've considered some challenging situations in the past few pages, things we have to face though we don't want to. They require quick techniques we can use in the moment. This last situation comes up less often, but it is extremely important and difficult when it does. Like the "Why am I here?" question about work, this situation calls for a technique that takes time and marshals your own genuine truth.

When You Have to Make a Tough Call and Both Choices Have Their Advantages

Sometimes decisions are easy. Shall I get dressed today? Sometimes they're a bit tricky. Should I take the subway or a shuttle to the airport? And sometimes they're downright thorny. Thai food tonight, or Italian? You need help with tough choices like this.

Okay, maybe you don't nee help with that last choice, but there really are times when tough choices present themselves, and you have to make a call when there are genuinely good reasons to go either way, or even one of three or four different ways. When such a truly difficult choice presents itself, you need to think big. Here is a wonderful way to unlock your real views, to find your real values in this situation. This comes to me from Sumi Loundon, the author of *Blue Jean Buddha*. She writes:

"I have recently begun employing a thought process that seems to work. In Buddhism, there are some practices that ask you to imagine yourself on your deathbed, completely letting go. To be honest, I don't know much about these practices, though I think they have something to do with learning about non-attachment. But for myself, when I am faced with an important decision, I imagine myself on my deathbed remembering my decision. . . . Try to picture yourself thirty years from now, or on your deathbed, remembering the decision you made as a young adult, and then think about whether you will like that decision or not."

An excellent method! What's so great about it is that the more important the decision—the higher the stakes—the easier it is to see what the right decision is. The key is really putting yourself in that imaginary position of looking back on today. It is easier to judge from there, since it's easier to use the right criteria.

May your deathbed be a long, long way away, and may you have that much more perspective to apply to your life now!

The simple brilliance of deciding "from your deathbed" is that it cuts right to the heart of what matters. It connects you with your real values—not the fleeting desires of the moment, but the honest needs that arise from our shared humanity.

In fact, this whole book is about bringing ourselves back to what matters. When we do so, we engage in the fundamental practice of being real and becoming even more real. As you read through this book and learn more of its solutions, you'll see more and more clearly how the process of becoming leads always away from illusory independence and toward a fundamental interconnectedness of all being. Buddhist teacher Thich Nhat Hanh calls this "interbeing." It's what we all truly are and what we all truly do.

2

Dealing with
Troublesome Types
(a.k.a., All Living Things)

SOME PEOPLE REALLY GET my goat. (I love that expression, though its origins are lost in time. Things arise and they pass away; we must not hold on too tightly) I'm talking about the troublesome types we encounter nearly every day, which is precisely why they're so nettlesome. If they were rarer, they wouldn't bug us so much because they'd be interesting curiosities that never got a chance to wear us down. If they were even more common, they again wouldn't bug us so much because we'd be used to them. As it is, there are just enough of them to keep us in a state of maximum irritation.

Have you noticed that when people talk about the wonder of this world and how it must have been created by God, then never talk about stuff like this? Instead they mention butterfly wings and babies' smiles and so on. They never get around to marveling at the creation of the mosquito or the insurance salesman. There may well be a God who created this world. If so, God is big enough to take credit for all things stale and suppurous as well as all things bright and beautiful.

On another level, each and every one of us can be a troublesome person. Just as all living things can be bodhisattvas or even Buddhas if we live up to our potential, so can we all be colossal jerks if we live down to our baseness. Guess which happens more often. Ah well, that's why we've got religions and governments and morals and parents—and helpful Buddhist books. One of those books says,

> Others' faults and errors are so plain,
> But our own are difficult to see.
>
> Dhammapada 252

Ain't that the truth! When someone brazenly takes the last hors d'oeuvre on the plate, doesn't it just, well, get your goat? I mean, who does he think he is? and what if the selfish jerk takes the last two?! Well, I'll tell you: I did that at a recent party, and people looked daggers at me. But you know why I did it? Because my pregnant wife was so famished she was nauseated and dizzy and had to sit down. She needed food and I got it for her. Was I at fault or committing an error, even though it looked so plainly like I was? So I ask: when you see the faults and errors in others, what are you really seeing? What do you really know? Expanding your view to include the unknown other, that is practice. That is cultivating compassion. That is living in non-duality. Or, if those sound too grand, it is just adding Buddha to your life.

In this chapter I'll give you some techniques to solve both sides of the troublesome people problem. They work on both sides because it's by acting like bodhisattvas that we best nullify the effect of jerks on us. So, in guiding you along the high road (acting like a bodhisattva), these techniques also help you on the low road (suffering fools graciously). In fact, it's in dealing with exactly these troublesome people where we get our best chances to make "spiritual" progress.

It sounds strange, but our adversaries, even our enemies, are our most consistent teachers. They are the folks we can count on to keep on showing us exactly where we're failing, where we're stuck, where we need to work on ourselves. And they sure come right at us with chances to do that work, bless their tiny, twisted hearts. One of my favorite Buddhist texts, the *Bodhicharyavatara* ("Guide to the Bodhisattva Life") puts a great deal of effort into teaching us how this happens. Here's one section:

> *And so, just like a treasure that arrives*
> *Without my having striven to attain it,*
> *I should be deeply happy with my enemies*
> *For they support my long awakening.*
>
> *Because they make me practice patiently,*
> *They are worthy of my giving them*
> *The flower of that patience: my compassion,*
> *For they have been the very cause of it.*
>
> Bodhicharyavatara 6.107-6.108

The author, Shantideva, points out something that only becomes obvious after we hear it. Our enemies deserve our thanks and our compassion precisely because we gain that compassion through having to deal with the likes of them! It's so difficult to gain compassion, we should be extra grateful they keep on giving us opportunities to do so. Our enemies are the cause of our progress. You can't get that from friends; they're too darn nice. Only enemies can be counted on to consistently help you out in this regard.

Alright then, our enemies are our friends. Good for them. But let's not be foolish: they're also still our enemies. The Buddha does not want us to be martyrs or doormats. We continue to strive for justice, equality, and all the rest.

> Just think of His Holiness the Dalai Lama, the exiled leader of Tibet. He has serious and implacable enemies: the Chinese government and its genocidal policies regarding Tibetan culture. His Holiness doesn't lay down for the Chinese, but neither does he hate them. He fights against them, but he does so in ways that always bring compassion to the fore. In fact, he's on record over and over praising the Chinese as his teachers. It's no coincidence that he also loves the *Bodhicharyavatara*.

Buddhism is not about giving up. It's just that, while we strive externally, we need to also marshal our inner resources to be open to learning from those we struggle against. Being open that way is tough and we can all use help getting there. In this chapter, I'll share some tricks I use to create that openness.

First let's consider troublesome people we don't know personally: telemarketers, politicians, bums, and terrorists. These are just examples, of course; I'm sure you have plenty of others we could add to the list. But the tricks that work with these folks will work with others. It's up to you to apply these tricks in your own dealings with your own nemeses.

After dealing with people we don't know, we move to people we do know. This is a more mixed bag, maybe not so awful, but also maybe less avoidable. (By the way: I'm saving the really maddening people—your loved ones—for later. They deserve their own chapter.) You're mostly stuck with people you know—your neighbors, bosses, teammates, and so on. You need responses to them that work within those relationships. You need responses that you can repeat over and over, that you can deepen, that in the end reshape those relationships.

Let's begin with people who inspire the rawest and most ignorant of emotions: hatred.

I Hate That #$%!

Admit it: hatred is exciting. People hate because on one level it feels good. It divides the world so simply. It psyches us up as "good guys" and reassures us there's a profound difference between us and the "evildoers." The fact that this is a load of crap does not enter into the equation; too messy. Hatred really does solve troubles. Unfortunately, it also creates new ones.

Do I need to tell you how hating traps you, brings you down to the level of the person you hate (or lower), steeps you in anger and bad emotions, repels everyone but other hateful people? No. You know all this already. You are the sort of person who buys this book. You are beyond hatred.

Okay, so you're not beyond hatred, but you want to be. Good enough, I'm there with you. How to get there? It's very quick, but, honestly, it does require effort.

Let's say you hate a coworker. This is not tough to imagine. We've all hated coworkers at one time or another. It's part of the job description. Take me. I hated the guy they hired for the full-time religion professorship at the university where I teach. I hated him for the obvious reason that he got the promotion and I didn't. So I just knew he was an idiot hired solely for the luck of having the same specialty as the retiring department chair. That pissed me off. Then he got more of my hatred by not single-handedly revamping the entire religious studies program as I, of course, would easily have done had they hired me. This was a perfectly detestable person.

Then I met him. End of hatred.

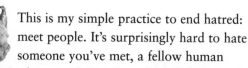 This is my simple practice to end hatred: meet people. It's surprisingly hard to hate someone you've met, a fellow human being. In fact, you'll find it so difficult that you'll give it up. This is my favorite form of spiritual practice: making it so hard to do the wrong thing that you just give in and do the right one out of laziness. We can use our own feeble human nature to improve ourselves.

This practice doesn't always work perfectly. Not everyone you hate turns out to be hip, humane, funny, and fearless in the face of bigotry the way my colleague did. Sometimes they turn out to be jerks. Fine. We are not talking about getting rid of annoyance here, we are talking about getting rid of hatred. Annoyance is life; hatred is a poison. You have to let it go, and the fact is that you often can let go of your burden of hating a guy even if he's a jerk when you see he's just stupid and frightened. It's genuinely difficult to hate frightened people, as it should be. When we find that jerks are jerks because they're afraid and don't have a better way of hiding it, then we can let go of our hatred of them. It's such a relief. Then we can move on to the long-term practice of dealing with them as flawed people.

I was even able to do this with the President!

I'm writing this book in 2004, but it's pretty much always necessary, no matter who's president. See them as fellow living beings, just as doomed as yourself. Then even their smugness doesn't seem so bad.

One key that turns up in several of these tricks to use with unknown people is to humanize the troublesome person. Humanizing them works because most of us are decent people, so when we see other people's humanity we relax, we open up to them, we might even begin to care about them. In any case, we let go of our reactive, negative mindsets—the immediate and stereotyped mode of experience we fall into when confronted by a situation we dislike. We fall into irritation, bias, and—so often—anger. It's ugly, and once we're there we feel trapped, unable to get ourselves out. Here's a classic instance in which almost all of us react with a negative mindset and need quick help.

How to Hang up on Telemarketers (Nicely)

You are just sitting down to dinner, or you're at the computer and the perfect solution to a problem at work has floated into your mind. Then the phone rings. It's hard to ignore such interruptions (it could be the lottery!). You answer, and a voice calls you by name (probably mispronouncing it) and asks you how you are. You make the error of answering. Now you're in for it, and you can't get a word in as you listen to a spiel for refinancing or vacation destinations or maybe, I don't know, hair polish, for the next two precious, irreplaceable minutes of your life. Your food or your brilliant idea grows cold as your frustration heats up. You can't seem to get away without being rude. What would Buddha do?

I used to say, "Thanks but I do not respond positively to any telephone solicitations, now matter how worthy. Good luck. Good bye." I would cling to the illusion that it would dissuade further calls from that person. Perhaps it does, but innumerable other callers exist.

I've recently starting a new practice, and I think Buddha would approve. My new practice is cleaner and simpler. I say: "Namu Amida Butsu! Goodbye," or "Om Mani Padme Hum! Goodbye," or "Bless you! Goodbye."

Now I don't claim to know if such blessings work on a cosmic level, but I can tell you this: they really do work on a personal level.

I did telephone survey work one summer. For a person who hated being rejected (and who doesn't?) it was horrible. Getting hung up on was a personal rejection, but at least it was quick. Professional phone workers, I learned, face a variety of worse things than being hung up on. Most involve people's unconscious projections and their need to act out when they know they're in a position of power. On the other hand, I did get a hot blind date once while I was doing a phone survey . . . but I digress.

When you bless a professional caller and hang up immediately and politely, you are truly blessing them. They can get on with their work, but more importantly, they have an instant of affirmation of connection with something greater, of relief from pressure and pain.

That blessing is easy to give. Start sending out your own quick blessing. You'll have plenty of opportunities!

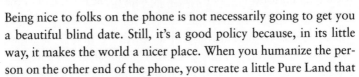

Being nice to folks on the phone is not necessarily going to get you a beautiful blind date. Still, it's a good policy because, in its little way, it makes the world a nicer place. When you humanize the person on the other end of the phone, you create a little Pure Land that the two of you inhabit for a time.

I mentioned in Chapter One how Pure Land Buddhists hope to be reborn in a place where becoming awakened will be much easier because things will be so nice and, well, pure. But now I seem to be saying that the Pure Land is right here, on this beat-up old planet of ours. What gives? Well, I don't claim to have the final say on the subject, but there are plenty of Pure Land folks who'll back me up when I ask, why not both? Maybe there's a Pure Land we can be reborn in. Excellent! On the other hand, maybe we can make this land we live in into a Pure Land too. Excellent again! Didn't Woody Guthrie write "This land is Pure Land, this land is my land"? Well, maybe not, but he had a vision of the great country of America becoming a whole lot greater through solidarity based on human respect. Woody was a great bodhisattva.

In individual ways we can create the Pure Land right here, right now. And when we work together, we create a lasting Pure Land on earth. This idea has been taught from the beginnings of the Pure Land school in China and is especially prevalent among Buddhists in Taiwan, like the hugely influential monk Hsing Yun and the incredibly successful nun Cheng Yen, whose Tzu Chi foundation has delivered effective aid all around the world.

Okay, we started small, with telemarketers who are intensely vexing but basically harmless. Now we'll go to the other end of the troublesome people spectrum. Politicians and terrorists can be not only intensely vexing but also deeply dangerous. Yet dealing with them calls for patience and humanization, just as dealing with telemarketers does.

When Politicians Make You So Angry You Can't Stand It

Was there ever a time when people weren't enraged by politicians? I can't imagine a politician that wasn't bone-headed or compromised, if not actually crooked. Still, politics is absolutely necessary. Consider the alternatives. Do you want anarchy? Fascism? Politics is inherent in democracy, so we need to treasure it. The trick is treasuring politicians too. It's like that old "Peanuts" cartoon where Linus says "I love mankind. It's people I can't stand." Here are two things I try. Well, I try the first. If that doesn't work, I do the second. It always works.

First, visualize as a bodhisattva the politician who makes you sick. Or, if you're Christian, visualize him as a saint. If you're Jewish, how about trying a miracle-working tzaddik? Pick your favorite religious role. Don't think about whether the politician *is* this wonderful being. On the practical level, of course they're not! This is a religious practice, not a political science class. But for just a moment, open yourself to this radical possibility. It helps to 1) shut your eyes for a second, 2) make the resolution in your mind, and 3) actually pretend there's a halo around them, or they're radiating pure light or their voice is like peaceful music.

When you see the politician like this, you'll create in yourself the softness of heart it takes to see where he or she is coming from. You'll open yourself to their potential. Your anger at them will fade away. Now you can decide whether their policies are worth voting for, listening to, or protesting against. Now you can change the world.

I confess, this trick sometimes doesn't work. Not mentioning any names, of course, but that bushy smirk is pretty darn hard to imagine on a bodhisattva. I suspect that, like me, you'll sometimes continue to feel anger, and you'll feel it's caused by this or that horrible politician and his or her horrible policies. Alright then, ready for the second deep and profound Buddhist practice? Here it is: change the channel, mute the sound, turn off the radio. Boom, problem solved.

I realize that sounds awfully simple. It *is* awfully simple, but that doesn't make it any less effective. A wonderful introduction to the dharma, the *Dhammapada*, begins with these renowned lines:

All things come at first from mind.
Mind creates them, mind fulfills them.
Speak or act with tainted mind,
You'll drag around a cart of pain.

When you keep watching a politician who taints your mind, you continue to drag around a cart of pain, which is . . . how shall I say . . . dumb. Cut it out. Let go of your pain and, as the scripture continues, "Speak or act with lucid mind / And joy will follow like your shadow."

This does not mean giving up your duty to change the world. It just means doing this from a place of wisdom, not anger.

Some people accuse Buddhism of being a passive religion, one that accepts too much and doesn't try to make the world a better place. Over the long history of Buddhism in Asia, there has been some truth in that accusation. In the last hundred years, though, things have been changing. Buddhists have been central to several Asian nations throwing off the shackles of colonization. And Buddhist principles still guide political progress in Asia today. Just consider the fact that two Nobel Peace Prize winners are Buddhist Asian leaders: His Holiness the Dalai Lama, leader of the Tibetan government in exile, and Aung San Suu Kyi, leader of the elected government of Burma, under house arrest for most of the last 15 years. In fact it was a Vietnamese monk, Thich Nhat Hanh, who invented the term "engaged Buddhism," meaning the kind of Buddhism that leaps into the fierce but compassionate struggle to make this world a better place for all living things—a way of being that engages every moment as the decisive moment in the struggle of peace and justice, in the heart and in the world.

We've just taken a quick look at how to combine compassion with politics. That's one aspect of engaged Buddhism. Here is another, even harder one.

What to Do When You Feel Like Bombing Terrorists Back to the Stone Age

Your country has just suffered another terrorist attack. The hapless cries of children run in blood down broken walls, while, on the other side of the world, other children dance for the joy of it. It's an outrage! You want to blow the terrorists up, blow them *all* up! What can end this rage? The release you feel with the release of bombs? No. Revenge merely buries rage; only pity ends it. But how do we feel pity for those who inflict terror and deal death?

 We must separate our feelings about the actions of terrorists from our feelings about terrorists themselves. See them as lost souls, hear them as crying infants, consider them as doomed fellow beings. My trick for this is simply to imagine in myself a pain so great it could lead me to kill. I imagine my suffering and rage at the killing of someone I love. When I feel that, I am feeling what a terrorist feels. Then I know the humanity of the terrorist and I don't have to hate him, only his actions.

This reversal can be hard, but it is magnificently simple and it gives me the freedom to separate evil actions from the pitiful persons who commit them. Once we make that separation, we can address the real root of terrorism: the harrowing situations in which it grows. Of course actually healing the hatred that breeds terrorism requires long and deep practice. That comes later. Start with the shattering moment of seeing the suffering terrorist.

Again, in this last example we see how political action flows from the root of compassion. Only when we get past the false image of the terrorist as inhuman can we get to the business of seeing where he really comes from. And only when we see the origins of terrorism in oppression can we effectively respond to and eradicate that place and thus terrorism itself.

Real change must come from compassion and work with wisdom. This is Buddhist politics. Anger only leads to more anger, as the state of the world shouts out to us every day. As the *Dhammapada* says, "Not by hate is hate defeated: / Hate is quenched by love. This is eternal law."

Compassion and wisdom are the two fundamental virtues in Buddhism. To function effectively and live happily, we must combine these two in our own lives. I've been describing situations where we do this with powerful persons we don't know. Such relationships are the substance of politics, where we're dealing with individuals we see but don't know, individuals with great power over us and the world. Now, though, let's shift our attention to persons without any power at all. These relationships, too, demand a balance between compassion and wisdom. Sometimes there's a real feeling of conflict between the two. I experience the following conflict several times a week, at least.

Giving the Bum a Buck

I live in L.A., so I'm always getting hit up for money when I'm in my car. If I lived in New York City I'd get hit up at the subway stairs. It's the same thing, though: I'm hurrying along, trying to fill up my tank or waiting at a freeway offramp, when some grubby guy gets in my face with a sign that says "Homeless. Will work for food," as if he thinks you constantly have little household chores you're not catching up on, and if you only could invite some homeless person over to attend to them your life would be so much easier. The guy knows this will never happen, so he's safe claiming he'd relish the opportunity to clean out your rain gutters.

Now, some homeless folks really do want to work and really do need food. There's no conflict here: give them something. You'll both feel immediately better when you do. Boom, you're Buddha! But you are most unlikely to find these folks on the freeway offramp. So let's talk about this other type, the guy who is not going to do any work anytime soon—not for you, not for anyone. This guy may have two or three places to choose from to get dinner tonight. Give him money and you can be sure it's not going toward a "Happy Meal." Fact is, his grubby little sign should probably say "I'm too messed up to work. I just want to drink my life away. Give me your money anyway." (I've actually seen signs that did say something like this. I admired their honesty.)

The deep practice here is to see the profound oneness between yourself and this unfortunate guy, to bow in gratitude to God or fate or karma for putting you in the car and him on the street when it might just as easily have been the other way around, to see your own face in his. This is the true formless giving of *dana*. Dana is the first of the Perfections of Buddhism. While there are different lists of Perfections for different schools of Buddhism, all of them, for all Buddhists, start with giving. Sadly for me and the folks who ask for my money, this deep practice almost always eludes me. Instead I do the shallow practice: I give the guy my change or my buck just to get him out of my face.

I admit that I find the problem of homeless people hard to face. I just can't stand being around the abject and miserable. You may feel like this, too. So what to do? Give the guy a buck and not only do you make him happy, you also make yourself happy in three ways:

1) You get to feel generous, if not actually compassionate. Hey, pat yourself on the back!

2) You get left alone. Whew!

3) You give the guy a chance to change. Sure, the chance that he'll change is tiny, but there's no chance at all while he's in need of a drink or a fix. Giving him that money is the only way you can help him in that one moment you're going to see him. He's got to want to change. He'll only do that when he's got some perspective, and he won't gain perspective until he gets whatever he's jonesing for. A brief respite from his need may give him a chance.

Good Buddhist practice is about creating the right conditions for change, so Buddha would say: Drop your judging and pick up your compassion! There will be plenty of time for judging later. For now, just cut the guy some slack and see what happens. You'll both feel better.

Feeling better is the bottom line of Buddhism. In fact, it's the bottom line of everything. We gauge—or at least we should gauge—the worth of actions, beliefs, and possessions by whether they make us feel better. Of course, from a Buddhist perspective "us" means more than just a collection of individuals; it means a larger "us" that includes those we love, those we share community with, and ultimately the whole world.

We do well to strive toward community. Think of what the word is made of: people living in common and in unity. Striving toward community takes time. In fact, it takes our whole lifetimes and many more. We're all working on it together. In the example of working with homeless people, we're looking at ourselves and other individuals; this is the individual level. On the larger, political level, the equivalent is working with masses of less fortunate people we'll never know, but who share the planet with us. These people are powerless compared to us, and they need a balance of our wisdom and our compassion.

Okay, so far we've looked at relationships with people we don't know and may never meet. Now I want to make the big shift to people we do know. I want to share a few means of increasingly community with people we see over and over, people whom we're stuck with. We'll start with one kind of person we should all be able to sympathize with, since we all are this person at one time or another.

When Someone Asks for a Favor They Don't Deserve

People are always asking for favors at the wrong times. They do it when we're swamped and don't have the time. Or they do it too often and the relationship gets imbalanced. We end up doing these calculations in our minds: Should I really put myself out for this person? Is it worth my time? Do they really deserve it?

The trick is to short-circuit that calculus. Favors are gifts, and gifts are undeserved by their very nature; otherwise they'd be payments. So naturally if we look at the small picture we don't find a reason to feel good giving a gift—or to feel comfortable receiving one. From such a limited perspective, we'd only feel right giving or receiving payments. But is that any way to live? I know it doesn't feel good when I live that way. I need to give more so I can feel good when I receive.

When you have the chance to give a gift or grant a favor, remember that giving is not just about the immediate reward to the other person. Giving is also about your own relationship to the world. As you give even a small amount, you slowly break down the artificial barrier between what is "me" and what is "not-me." That's why Mahayana philosophers talk about there being no giver and no receiver. Sure, in this moment you are one, but this moment is not separate from another moment when you'll be the other. The mind you create now will lead to the mind you have then. From such a perspective, all elements involved are inseparable: no giver, no gift, no receiver. When you can embody that unity, you are practicing pure giving.

Until then, try this: when someone asks you for a favor, just say "yes," without hesitating and without thinking. Don't make any room for equivocation or evaluation. Say yes first and think later. I often urge you to think about things differently to help your practice, but this time I'm telling you not to think at all. You don't necessarily want to engage in not-thinking every single time someone hits you up for a favor. But it's a wonderful practice to do every now and then. With repetition, you'll break down the tension between giving and paying that taints ordinary giving. You'll slowly approach the freedom of pure giving.

There is always going to be some conflict when others ask you for favors—at least until you become a tenth-stage bodhisattva, which is not likely to be any time soon. Sorry. Accept that and let yourself feel good about giving when you give. After all, there are worse things than feeling conflicted about giving to someone. There is, for instance, feeling you want to slug someone. Oh yes, you feel that way sometimes. I know you do. How? Because I feel it too.

Faced with certain people who want certain inimical things, anger arises. Tensions escalate. Tempers flare. Fights happen. This process is going to happen to you, to me, to all of us. We accept that the process will arise because anger will arise. The trick, then, is to arrest the process. I'm going to give you two ways to halt and even reverse it.

How Fights Happen and How You Can Defuse Them

Imagine you're at a party, talking with an acquaintance about families, and somehow the topic of abortion comes up. That person says some horribly unfeeling thing. You begin to get upset. You blurt out your passionate feeling. The other person gets hotter and says something so stupid, so intentionally hurtful, that you are simultaneously incensed and driven to fix him or her. This kind of thing is especially prone to happen if there's alcohol involved, but alcohol is not the problem. It happens at work, too, where there's no alcohol, only human beings. Some bozo thinks he knows better than you how to organize a meeting, write a memo, or install widgets; you starting arguing, and you just have to win.

I like to win verbal arguments as much as the next guy. But it's almost always pointless, and I've managed to get to a point where I can stop myself. I still want to be right, but I stop fighting to be right, and I do it by concentrating on exactly that feeling of wanting to win.

When I realize I'm in a fight, when I feel anger and a drive to win, I take one second to feel the intensity of my need to be right and win. I then place that intensity in the head of my opponent. That allows me to feel how much winning means to them, too. As I wish to win, so does my opponent. Immediately, I lose much of my desire to defeat them. It's not that I don't want to be proven right; it's just that I don't want to harm someone so much like me.

Feel the intensity of your own anger and drive. See that in your opponent. Know you are the same. Feel yourself relax. Sometimes this is even a little bit funny; you'll find yourself shaking your head at yourself. That's okay.

While we're on the subject, let's consider . . .

Another Way to Defuse a Fight

We can only fight effectively with someone close to our own level. Someone below us isn't a strong enough enemy, while someone above us is too strong (and may find us too weak). So, if you feel a fight coming on, stop the process by getting rid of the even fighting ground.

Suppose you're fighting with a co-worker over a problem that's not getting dealt with and is getting worse. The stakes might be high for both of you. With the high stakes come high tensions that easily warp into anger. When you feel that anger and know you're about to say or do something hurtful, instead raise up your co-worker as you would a sacred image such as a Buddha. Visualize lifting that person right up into the purity of the heavens, where the clear mind of light will pour through him and maybe give him some sense for once. You are lifting him up and simultaneously prostrating yourself. After all, that person is the Buddha, or could be, so there's no sacrilege.

The part about lowering the self is easier. In the middle of a fight, when you can't even manage to think of your enemy's needs and sufferings, just bow. Yes, a full prostration would look a trifle odd, especially if, say, you're mad at the grocery clerk or the meter maid. But you can bow your head. Your opponent may may think you're just too disgusted to look at him or her. That may even be true. But the very act of bowing, of letting yourself relax, of lowering your level of hostility, changes your inner world. You break the chain of anger and open yourself to the kernel of Buddhahood inside the other. Just bow inside and let what happens happen.

My two tricks for defusing fights are not completely separate. After all, in Buddhism nothing is completely separate. You might find yourself lowering your head just as you accept and feel your anger at the other. But if you try both tricks, do them one after the other, not both at once. The first is primarily mental, the second primarily physical. Of course the mental effects the physical and vice-versa, but each has its own energies, and those energies are best focused on one at a time. For me, seeing my opponent as myself works better first. Then I'm in good shape to raise him like a Buddha. Try that order. In this way you're also bowing to yourself and thus giving yourself a little credit for simply being nice and trying to learn from a difficult situation. That's hard practice and you deserve that bow.

I find another situation even tougher than avoiding fights in the first place. It has to do with anger, and though I'm not really an angry guy, I am proud and judgmental. Pretty un-Buddhist, I know, but I have to level with you: I want to be the best, and I can't stand getting criticized. I want to be the best without effort, simply as a natural expression of my greatness. But to be honest, I can barely learn a thing without criticism. I need help. We all do. Yet help comes often through criticism, and we're so reluctant to accept it. It's a pickle. Here's how I encourage myself to escape it.

Getting Criticized without Getting Angry

We all know that creepy feeling that seems unstoppable: you've done your job or made your play or said your piece, and then someone jumps on you. Maybe they have a point, maybe they don't, but that doesn't matter to your feeling. The feeling says "No no no!" The feeling says "Shut up!" The feeling says "Fuck you!" And the feeling fills you with energy and the illusion of power and righteousness.

We all hate being criticized, and that hate mobilizes powerful energies in us without asking us first. It simply happens as soon as our inner voice starts saying "You don't understand! It wasn't like that! You're an idiot!" The noise is so immediate and so loud that sometimes we don't even hear the actual critique if our poor critic doesn't get it out fast enough. How do we break open our defensive mind so we can actually hear and therefore learn from criticism instead of just hearing the sound of our own righteous inner monologue?

Here's the process:

1) Breathe. Focus your attention on your breath for just one inhale. Okay, maybe an inhale and an exhale. This reminds you there's more going on with you than the critique addresses. Is anyone criticizing your breathing? No. Why? Because your breathing kicks ass.

2) Add a verbal reminder of the larger context. You are more than the little debate that's going on. A quick and powerful phrase is what you need here—in effect, a mantra. Choose one that works for you. Perhaps "I am more than this." I talk more about this highly useful mantra in Chapter Five.

3) Now turn your attention back to the criticism; you've made room in yourself to see that it doesn't threaten you. And you probably haven't even missed anything; the whole process of breathing and repeating your mantra only took five or ten seconds, max. If you did miss something, you are now ready to engage it. Just ask your critic to repeat it. Tell them you want to make sure you understand what they're saying. They will not only be happy to oblige, they might also be a bit shocked. They may very well soften some of their own edge and offer you a more constructive critique. But that's a bonus you can't count on. What you can change is your own conduct and your own experience, and that you've already done. You're ready to learn.

How about that? You made it through this particularly tough chapter. This was probably the darkest chapter in the book and you've passed through it. Congratulations! I say, give yourself a well-deserved rest. Think about what you've read. And remember, your next chance to practice might be just a ringing phone away.

Yes, the next chapter also has its challenging moments. Remember when I said I was saving your really maddening loved ones for later, since they deserve their own chapter? Well, that chapter is next. But those moments are counterbalanced by the unending richness our loved ones give our lives. No matter how troublesome they can be, we still don't label them "troublesome people." Usually we just give up on labels, which are too weak to describe the hugeness of these beloved and benighted persons in our lives.

Love: The Root of All Evil— oops, sorry, I mean "Love: What Makes Life Worth Living"

OUR MADDENING LOVED ones balance that madness they add to our lives with the richness they add as well. I want to say more about that. In fact, this entire chapter presents a series of situations saying more about that.

Naturally part of the title is a joke: there's no way love really makes life worth living. (Ha! Sorry, that was a joke, too.) Truly, I believe that love is exactly what makes life worth living; a life without love is simply too sad to contemplate. It's not really even "life," it's more like "pre-death." Let me quickly add, too, that the love that makes life worth living does not have to be romantic love. It doesn't even have to be human love: there are millions of people whose love for animals or nature or God gives plenty of depth and meaning and joy to their lives.

No, the joke part of the title was that love is the root of all evil. I'm playing on the biblical line that suggests money, or, more exactly, the love of money, is the root of all evil. But the love of money is not the same as the love of people. Love of money is greed and cannot be satisfied; it's an endless wheel of desire and frustration. Love of people is pure love; it is always satisfied because it asks for nothing beyond itself. It wants to give, not to take. Such love symbolizes and embodies all that is sacred in humanity, and that is why I say it makes life worth living.

The trick, of course, is keeping that pure love alive in the face of the thousand natural shocks that it is heir to. Love is one thing; being and staying in love is another thing altogether. To keep love alive, and, better, to nurture it to greater heights, demands work. That work ultimately pays off for everyone, but it's still work. This chapter will give you ways of doing that work more efficiently so that the payoff comes more quickly and more handsomely.

Let's first look at annoyances caused by family members—the only people we can never escape, because we carry them around in our genes and our pasts and futures. Here I include a couple situations involving the previous generation and a couple involving the next. Past, present, or future, it's all in the family. . . .

On the Phone with A Tedious Parent

Imagine you're trying to finish up the day's work so you can get going on dinner or maybe make it to that movie you've been wanting to see, but the phone rings at just the wrong time. It's your mom, who launches into a long tirade about her glaucoma or arthritis or hair salon problems. This is—well, let's just say it's intensely annoying. Yes, we have all been there.

The Buddha taught us to repeat a vow: "Once I was supported by them; now I will be their support. I will perform the duties they performed and maintain the family and its traditions. I will preserve my inheritance and make myself worthy of my heritage." I wouldn't repeat such a lengthy string of words, and I don't expect you to. What matters to me is what works, and what works is the thought behind the words. We repeat vows because they so powerfully re-create and empower our intentions when we need it at times like this.

Try a vow. Just repeat in your mind, in your own words, a short reminder of what you owe your mom—something like, oh, I dunno, maybe "I owe you my life; I owe you my life; I owe you my life."

Put that thought into your head. Don't worry about what your mom might be saying while you're thinking it. You can listen to yourself and her at once, and, anyway, you're probably not missing anything new or vital. You are simply replacing "You are so te-dious" with "I owe you my life." The effect can be startling.

Let me quickly add that my mother is not really like that. In fact, the Tibetan Buddhist practice of generating compassion and love for other people by thinking of them as your mother from a previ-ous life works particularly well for me because I have so much love for my mother in this life. Still, any person can be tedious, and I've heard that parents can be particularly so. Mobilize the love you feel, even in tedium.

Okay, now for something completely different (and yet which eventually leads to something exactly the same, one generation later). This time, you're the parent, not the child. This time you're controlling the situation—or are you?

When You're Tempted to Give in to Your Child after Saying Otherwise

Imagine you're at a play date. Your son has had a good time all afternoon and is still happy being there. Now, however, you have to leave so you can still make it to the dry cleaner before you go home. You tell Junior it's time to leave. Junior resists leaving. Junior says "*NO!*" Junior is very candid and free in his dealings with you. But how are you with him? He's simple; he knows what he wants. You're complex and conflicted; what do you want? What to tell him? You don't feel like telling him how you forgot to pick up the clothes yesterday and now you need them before tomorrow night but you don't think you can make it there tomorrow. You don't want to get into all that. What would he care, anyway? You are an adult and need to balance various needs and desires; he's a kid and just wants what he wants, right now. As you think about it, you realize you could probably pick up the clothes during lunch, tomorrow, and your husband could wear his shirt two days in a row. . . .

And at this point, I can hear the Buddha saying "*STOP!*" The Buddha sees the fundamentals and goes right to the point. Say he asks you, "Have you told Junior it is time to go?" If you say "yes," you can just about hear the Buddha reply, "Then it is time to go. If you stay now, you will have lied to your child. No good will come of that."

 There are big issues and conflicts at play in this situation. I can't analyze them all for you. I'm just pointing out the basics, as always, and it doesn't take a Buddha to see what's most important here. You've said it is time to go, now you must back up your words. Your honesty and your child's confidence in it are the foundation of your relationship and of your child's entire future. What is more important, five more minutes on the swing set or staying true to your word?

It's a tough situation, since we are genuinely torn in it and there is no solution that completely avoids pain. Well, isn't that a surprise? Dukkha rears its head again. Choose one way and you create immediate dukkha. Choose the other way and you just postpone it. Which is the wiser path? The honest one.

This certainly does not exhaust the theme of parenting. In fact, authors have written whole books on Buddhist approaches to being a parent and raising children. We can't do that here—we've got all of life to cover—but let's consider another variation on the theme. If you have kids, or even if you just know any kids, you'll recognize it.

Do You Buy the Kid Ice Cream or Not?

You're at the zoo. It's fun, of course. If you don't like zoos, I think you're not a very well-adjusted mammal. You and the kid are having a good time, but when she walks by the ice cream stand she is seized with an irresistible urge to consume, consume, consume. This is no surprise; she is programmed by her genes and her society to feel this. If you say "yes" to her, you create pleasure. If you say "no," you create pain. Seems an easy choice, but it's not because really you're faced with a choice between short-term and long-term happiness. You must decide, and your decision will vary depending on the occasion. You could get into a whole deep discussion with your kid each time you walk by an ice cream/candy/churros/nuts/popcorn/whatever stand. That would be laudable in a way, but it would also be a serious amount of work for you and *way* too much work for your child.

Here's something simpler: put yourself in her stomach. Is it empty in there? If you've eaten at the same time as your kid, you know as soon as you put attention on your own stomach. If your kid ate separately, just feel how long it's been and how hungry he or she must be. This gives you all the information you need to make a quick and definite decision. You can throw in the "How much junk food do I want my child to eat?" question, but that's a whole new level of complexity. Start with simple meal timing.

This is not a test of wills or a battle over who is boss, unless you make it one. You are the boss, and you are deciding an issue of what and when to feed your child. Stay with the fundamentals.

The trouble comes when we lose touch with fundamentals. Especially in upwardly mobile families, where both parents are away at work a lot, there's a tendency to want to make up for absence by saying "yes" to whatever children want. When this happens, we lose sight of the fundamental relationship between parents and children. Kids slowly get the uneasy feeling that they might be the bosses. That's not what kids really want, and they'll react to it in any number of ways, all bad. They might look like they're enjoying the extra stuff they get, but the deeper confusion they feel is too steep a price for them to pay. All parents want to please their kids, so all of them are in danger of falling, along with their kids, into this trap. You need to short circuit the cycle, tough as that is when you first start.

How simple the solution is! How difficult to accomplish! We shouldn't be surprised about this. It is so difficult because it goes straight to the heart of human nature. We are wanting machines. We want, want, want. And no amount of getting, getting, getting stops the wanting, wanting, wanting. We are happier when we learn this truth, though many of us never do.

As parents, we have the greatest opportunity to help other beings learn this truth. Gratifying your child's every wish will not get the job done. What would that teach? Even if you could somehow accomplish it for a time, what would happen later?

The Buddha taught us to find happiness in relationships, not things. He taught that we ourselves *are* relationships, not things. Teach your child the same. There's a middle path between indulgence and denial, and that path works for kids as well as adults. You are your child's compass and teacher; as you decide a middle path for yourself, you must decide it for her. You'll be teaching the most important lesson in life: to look for happiness not in gratification but in the eternal flow of relationships.

Speaking of relationships . . .

A child's relationship to her or his parents is not only the first but the most powerful and influential relationship in life. What we there learn of love, we do not forget—even though we might wish it. What is done to us, we do ourselves; and what we do at first, we repeat all our lives. Yes, we can change, but we change only from a strong base. If that base is insecure, our work to change is never finished. Sometimes the best solution is to turn away entirely.

Just Say No

No, this is not about sex. This is about the pain of bad relationships. There are many types, but let's look at dealing with bad parents. I don't mean parents who occasionally annoy you. Unless your parents are Mary and Joseph (and I'm talking about *the* Mary and Joseph, if you know what I mean), they occasionally annoy you. That annoyance is right and normal. I'm talking about parents who sometimes really mean ill to you, and who always drive you to distraction. I'm talking about parents who may still love you in their strange way, but their love is not expressed positively and their relationship with you can only add to your dukkha. To such persons, you may have to just say "no." "No," I do not want to come spend Thanksgiving listening to you berate me. "No," I will not get in between you and your landlord again. "No," I am not going to accept the blame for your frustrated life. Just say "no."

This is a very sad thing, of course. But perhaps no sadder than the actual time you spend together. If this is so, you simply need to limit or stop your exposure to such parents (and to anyone else this description fits). Just saying "no" ends power games that may be too painful to continue.

Such relationships are like harmful mind states. The Buddha gives us meditative practices to curtail them. Just as in meditation you replace harmful mind states with helpful or neutral ones, so you have the power to replace harmful relationships with helpful or neutral ones. If you can just say no to power dynamics that cause pain, you can potentially transform your harmful relationship to a helpful one. This is extremely difficult, because not only do you have to start the process, the other person has to engage it as well. If that other person can't or won't, the relationship ends. Then it is at least neutral, and that's fine, too.

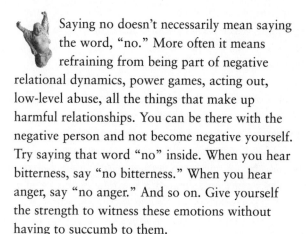 Saying no doesn't necessarily mean saying the word, "no." More often it means refraining from being part of negative relational dynamics, power games, acting out, low-level abuse, all the things that make up harmful relationships. You can be there with the negative person and not become negative yourself. Try saying that word "no" inside. When you hear bitterness, say "no bitterness." When you hear anger, say "no anger." And so on. Give yourself the strength to witness these emotions without having to succumb to them.

Most of us, thank goodness, do not have to take such drastic measures with our parents. But just about all of us find ourselves in a similarly awful relationship at least once in our lives. We have to remember that relationships change. When we change or end one, we become a new person. This is surely scary. It is also empowering.

Let's take a little break now and turn to a happier side of relationships. Loved ones drive us crazy, but not all the time. Now let's look into the most important relationships of our adult lives: our relationships with partners. . . .

Taking the "Game" out of the Dating Game

Ah, the dating game. I remember it well—and thank God the clock on my dating game has expired! Dating is always a game in the sense of being something you do with others, don't know the outcome of, and really want to win. But dating should not be a game in the sense of being "just a game," something unreal and unrelated to the serious parts of life.

Imagine a date where you're just meeting this person or have only met them once or twice before at parties or school or work or wherever. You don't know each other, and it's easy to succumb to the temptation to pretend a bit during the date. You may want to act like a player, a cupcake, a daredevil, a hottie, or a cool dude. This can be fine, at first, but it can get awkward as time goes on. It's one thing to be daring on a first date and take chances you normally wouldn't. It's another if you make stuff up to support your pose and then have to keep it up even though it's not your real self. You might embellish your outdoor enthusiasm, for instance. But what happens when your date whisks you away on a surprise trip and says "Hey, thanks for pumping me up. Guess what? We're headed to the mountains to take on the Class V rapids on White Death River! Awesome, huh! I'm depending on you to get us through Neckbreaker and Devil's Chute alive!"

Okay, that's funny and unlikely. But what if you've made him think you're the strong, silent type, when inside you're just crying out for a hug? That's a little closer to home, huh? What do you do then? Suck it up? Admit you're a fake? This is a game you can't win. Lie to your date and you lie to yourself. We find ourselves, we *become* ourselves in relationship. So our intimate relationships are us. If we lie in those relationships, who are we? We're false, unreal. Real freedom is the freedom to be authentic. Only in authenticity lie genuine happiness and contentment.

 Instead of lying on your dates, try radical honesty. Anyone worth being with is just about as nervous about being honest as you are. Break through that nervousness by sharing something radically true but not directly related to the relationship. You're interested in Buddhism. Start there. Describe why you read this book and what you got out of it. Just say a few sentences, but real ones, ones that reveal your own search to find who you are. Then wait for— in fact, demand—a real response. You'll be creating the basis for a genuine relationship. Or if not, at least you'll find out quicker there's no "there" there.

Ah, so the dating game is not such a "game," after all. To enter that game, to be a genuine player—not a "player"—is to open yourself to honesty and the places it can take you. You can maybe tell I was never much of a dater, even in high school. I was a pretty serious guy and I missed out on some things (mostly sex). And yet, appreciating where my honesty has taken me, I wouldn't change it. Decide for yourself, but know that the Buddha took the honest path.

Okay, let's say you have been honest—as much as any of us can be—and you've ended up in a real relationship. In fact, you've ended up in the sack. Here's a quick tip on find more intimacy there.

Deepening Your Sex Life

You are making love. You feel excitement in your loins. It's like a vibration, yet it's also a rush that carries you along. It pushes you into your partner. It feels irresistible, like a wave engulfing you. Having sex is bodysurfing that wave. You push yourself into it, then it just carries you away—yet you can always pull out. The power, the desire, feels outside you, but it's really inside. Can you remain aware of this? If you can, your awareness adds a new dimension to your sexuality.

People say they get carried away by the excitement of sex. Yes, but this can trap them in their solo experience and can lead to actions they come to regret. It's also not the whole story. In fact it is our highly focused awareness of our physical and fantastical interaction with the wave of sexual excitement that makes it continue. In fact, we create the wave, and we sustain it. Though it has its own power, we can also shape that wave and deepen it.

As a simple practice to deepen your sexual experience, look into your partner's eyes during sex. This will bring you into awareness of your co-creation of the moment. See yourself and your partner together. Good sex is mutual; it is a place where body and mind and giving and receiving all come together.

This is why high-level tantric practitioners can and do engage in sex as spiritual practice. In the mutuality of sex, they try to embody—literally and fully—*anatman*, the fundamental non-separateness and relatedness of persons.

Advanced spiritual sex is deep practice, very challenging and very complicated, but simple togetherness in sex is not nearly so complex. Start with simply looking in your partner's eyes. Tantric sex is not for everyone, but being together is. Really look and let yourself be looked into. It may open a path to something deeper.

Now let's return to the world of difficulty, "annoyance of everyday life." That's the world of this book's title, and it's where we need to focus our attention if we want to ever make any progress in fundamental practice.

Alright then. Imagine the lovemaking is past and you and your partner have managed to find something to fight about. As you know, this doesn't exactly take a genius to envision.

Yelling at Your Partner

Let's say you're fighting with your husband. God *damn* can he be pigheaded when he wants to be! (Note to the reader: any resemblance to actual persons, living or dead, is strictly coincidental.) You start out with a simple dispute about something practical, but within about 30 seconds the thing gets away from you. You don't know where it comes from, and right now that doesn't matter, it's just there. Really there. You are shouting because he won't listen when you speak, and he is shouting for the same reason. Maybe you were right about the original issue, maybe not, but now you're talking trash about him, not about the issue. What the hell are you doing? How do you resolve this argument?

Here's the reality: you don't. Once you reach the place of personal attack, you are not getting back to the point until you just shut up. And, voilà!, there's your practice: shut up. Shut the hell up.

I mean this literally. When you're in a fight with your partner, you are in hell. When you shut up, you shut hell up. Do it! Shut that damned door! In the silence that follows, you are still angry. Of course you are! But let the silence in. Even if he's still yelling, you can let the silence in. You've got a space in which to breathe now. Yes, just breathe for a moment. Your breathing is always there, always available to steady you. You can now go on to tougher work: separating your anger from your argument, separating your relationship from your issue, separating both of your characters from your positions. Hard work, indeed, but it's the work you need to do, and you can only begin it once you shut up.

The Buddha called for Right Speech and made it part of the Eightfold Noble Path, the fundamental way to be Buddhist, since the very beginning. You can think of shutting up as the preamble to Right Speech. In fact, in one of the earliest Buddhist texts, Right Speech is two-thirds no-speech:

1) If it's false, harmful, and nasty, don't say it.
2) If it's false, harmful, and pleasant, don't say it.
3) If it's false, helpful, and nasty, don't say it.
4) If it's true, harmful, and nasty, don't say it.
5) If it's true, helpful, and nasty know when to say it.
6) If it's true, helpful, and pleasant know when to say it.

That's clear, right? Out of six types of things to say, only two should be said, the two that are both true and helpful. And you should only say them if you know when to do it. Any other time they will just blow up in your face (and the other person's). It all boils down to one fundamental rule:

When in doubt, shut up. Thus have I heard.

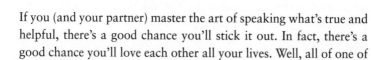

If you (and your partner) master the art of speaking what's true and helpful, there's a good chance you'll stick it out. In fact, there's a good chance you'll love each other all your lives. Well, all of one of your lives. Even if you never break up, one of you will lose the other to death.

People sometimes accuse me of being morbid, but I'm just being honest—without even mentioning the other possibility, that both partners die together in some horrible accident. Now that would be morbid. Oh, oops; I've mentioned it.

When faced with loss, we all need to grieve. That is, we need to honestly face the loss and our legitimately rotten feelings about it. This is not indulgent. Nor is it avoidable. It's just dukkha.

Though Lovers Be Lost, Love Shall Not

We've all felt the pain of losing people we love—sometimes because we grow apart and leave, sometimes because we grow old and die. Loss is unavoidable. There's no magic Buddhist protection sphere I can offer you. I'm sorry. But I can present you with this: grief is inseparable from joy. Grief is the experience of remembering past joy as lost. But such joy is not lost. It's right there inside you, and your grief proves it.

We're sad at losing someone because we miss old moments we spent together. But those beautiful old moments only happened because we were immersed in them, because we weren't sitting around missing even older moments. It is exactly the absence of the past that makes the present possible.

To free yourself of the past, you must grieve. Grief is okay. Cry. Grieve. Feel that pain, do not hide from it, do not judge it. Humans are naturally self-healing. That's just as true for grief as it is for, say, bones. When you break a bone you don't prevent healing by experiencing the pain. In fact feeling the pain tells you what not to move, what not to put weight on, what position to take to heal fastest, and so on. This happens naturally because we aren't able to interfere with bone healing. We *can* interfere with emotional healing, and this can slow or even stop it. So just experience the pain of grief. Let your tears wash you clean of it. This is how, after loss, we open ourselves to the present.

But if your grief is trapping you, try this exercise:

 When you feel the sadness of loss, change your emotion by looking into its root. Ask yourself: What did I have with that lost person that I don't have now? Be specific about a quality or an event you experienced with them. Now, let yourself relive that quality or experience. Go ahead. This is not indulgence as long as you don't let it stop you from moving forward in your life, and if you're so sad you're not involved in your life now, you really need to do this exercise to reawaken yourself. Feel how good it was to be with that person in that moment. Do you feel it? Then you still have it! That pleasure you feel is the same pleasure. Your grief is also a celebration. You carry the past with you, always. As Dylan Thomas wrote, "Though lovers be lost, love shall not."

Life/death, love/grief, now/then. All are inseparable. We love the first halves of these pairs, but without the second halves there are no first halves, and even in the second halves the first halves endure. This is our world: irredeemably split, unendingly one.

Ah playing with language! But language is not a toy. Language has real power over us, whether we're aware of it or not. There are times we acknowledge this and use its power to empower ourselves. One example is repeating our marriage or partnership vows. As we repeat them, we allow them to change us. When I said "I, Franz, take you, Nina, to be my wife," those words changed me from bachelor to husband, and that change gave me greater power to be a good husband. That's serious power. Now I want to show you one way to return that power to your life.

What Vows Are For

Imagine you're fighting with your partner. Let's call him a him, though it could just as easily be a her. Both sexes have been known to fight. You're fighting about who's been worse in dealing with the car maintenance. Or, even better, you're fighting about the way he snidely implied that you've been slack, while he's fighting about your infuriating attempts to play the sensitive one in these fights. After just a few moments, the fight isn't even about the car anymore; it's about the fight itself. This is so pointless and yet so common.

When I find myself in a fight like this, I realize I'm not even listening to what my wife is saying to me. She may be shrill (and I may be self-righteous), but her shrillness doesn't matter if I'm not even hearing what she's saying. She could be a harpy or a saint; it doesn't matter when I've tuned her out. The fight can continue indefinitely with both sides yelling their internal monologues at each other.

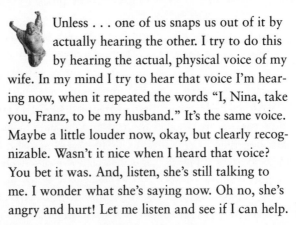Unless . . . one of us snaps us out of it by actually hearing the other. I try to do this by hearing the actual, physical voice of my wife. In my mind I try to hear that voice I'm hearing now, when it repeated the words "I, Nina, take you, Franz, to be my husband." It's the same voice. Maybe a little louder now, okay, but clearly recognizable. Wasn't it nice when I heard that voice? You bet it was. And, listen, she's still talking to me. I wonder what she's saying now. Oh no, she's angry and hurt! Let me listen and see if I can help.

It doesn't always work quite so swiftly as that, but tuning in to the remembered and treasured sound of her voice reminds me of what we share and what gives me the greatest joy on earth. I can then begin to hear the specific words she's saying now and accept them as part of the package. Hearing your partner's old voice will also bring to mind your own, saying "I, _____, take you, _____, to be my _____." That will help you harmonize your tone with your love.

I keep coming back to the difficulties and the rewards of relationship. This doesn't surprise you, does it? In relationship, and only in relationship, we exist. We become who we are, and we make our contribution to the future, the next generation.

Still, not all relationships are worth being in. Some simply create too much dukkha. As with parents, sometimes with partners the best thing is to cut the ties that bind. The process of making this decision is always wrenching and staggeringly difficult. There is no way around that, nor should there be. It's supposed to be hard to break up, and it's always hard to stay together. Here is one little practice to help you.

Your Relationship: Frustrating or Exhausting?

Should you continue your relationship? Should you give up on relationships altogether? I'm at the point in life where I'm realizing that some of my friends will never be married. They've effectively given up the chase. For years this was hard for me to understand. But recently I've come to see this decision as simply one of many possible decisions about love, as valid as any of the others. What makes this decision, or any other, correct is insight into our selves and our dukkha.

Should you put effort into finding or preserving a relationship? This question never goes away. As we change (which we always do), every one of us needs to ask the questions and honestly face our inner response. Even old married folks need to ask it. There's no shame in that. In fact, there's great power. If your relationship feels exhausting, it's in trouble. But if it feels frustrating, there's hope.

Have you been to this place? You're on the rocks with your lover. You fight all the time, and when you're not fighting you feel distant from each other. Let's say you're deciding what movie to go see. You think he wants to see some dumb buddy picture, and he thinks you want to see some treacly chick flick. Damned if you're going to go see guys blowing each other up, and damned if he's going to sit through two hours of sappy soundtrack. As you argue, you can't bring yourselves to look at each other.

Bad scene. What is really going on here? You're frustrated because you want to put effort into the relationship and don't know how. You're frustrated because that dammed up energy has to come out, and it comes out in anger. When trivial issues seem important, something else is the real issue. Turn your attention to that.

Look inside. Feel your anger. Visualize streaming it out at your lover, really hitting and scratching and biting. Does that make you feel better? Now visualize streaming it out at "the relationship," at the fight you're having. Does that make you feel better? If the first makes you feel better, then you need to reevaluate the worth of this relationship. If the second makes you feel better, then you're frustrated and need to find ways of rechanneling your energy into the relationship. Sure, that sounds bad, but it's really good: you've got the energy to do the work.

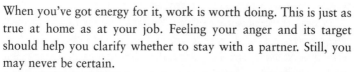

When you've got energy for it, work is worth doing. This is just as true at home as at your job. Feeling your anger and its target should help you clarify whether to stay with a partner. Still, you may never be certain.

I wish I could offer you a totally reliable, 100-percent fool-proof way of finding certainty in relationships. I can't give you one because there is no such thing in human life. It is a fundamental quality of us humans: our not knowing. We so often just don't know if our choices are smart or right. Faced with this doubt in such a vital aspect of our lives, what should we do? Don't just throw up your hands or acquiesce to what's easiest. Here's one more trick to turn a problem into an opportunity.

When You Don't Know if This Marriage Is the Right Thing After All

You love your partner. I know you do. But there are times when any loved person who's that close to us, who's that inevitable and that inevitably different from us, is going to be intolerable, without even meaning to, just by his or her very presence. When that happens—whether it's because she just can't resist criticizing your driving, or he won't lift a damned finger to clean the garage, or neither one of you can be the one to take the first step and apologize for last night—there's the deadening worry that maybe the whole relationship was a terrible mistake, that your whole life has been wasted.

That is why I love the place in the *Tannisho* where Shinran, the founder of Jodo Shinshu Buddhism, basically says "Darned if I know whether I'm making spiritual progress! It's quite possible I'm actually headed straight to hell. But since I'm not able to do any of those deep practices that would surely save me, I'll just do the little things I can. We'll see how it turns out."

What's the connection between Shinran's religion and our marriage? Marriages are like religions. We commit to them, and they uphold and sustain us. They may also shape, even distort us. But they're our practice. They're who we are. And we don't ever know for certain if they're right.

There you have it: just as Shinran can't tell if he's going to hell, we can't tell if our marriages are. Yet just as Shinran keeps on practicing and is deeply grateful for his practice, so should we be grateful in our marriages. Shinran knows he's not capable of any totally glorious, wonderful, exalted practices. That's like us knowing we're not going to have totally glorious, wonderful, exalted partners. Shinran teaches us to live honestly, so does marriage.

You have to love Shinran's combination of humility and stubbornness. That's exactly what we need in marriage, too. In the end, the two lead to real bliss. So when the moment is black and you doubt your wedded path, be like Shinran; just say, "I'm not in any other marriage, I'm in this one. And I don't have to know if it's right." Let go of knowing; this is a question without an

answer. Knowing is boring, anyway. Love your
life. Live your marriage.

I use the word "marriage" in this scenario because marriage is
the most decisive of relationship choices, but the same advice holds
for any committed relationship. It's just as true for civil unions as it
is for religious ones. It's just as true for same-sex partners as it is
for opposite-sex partners. And it's just as true for business partners
as it is for romantic partners. It's all about commitment to honesty
and humbleness.

The idea of not knowing fills most of us with dread: What if we're
wrong! But it fills some of us with passion: What freedom to
change! It helps explain why the Zen Peacemaker Community has
taken this passionate freedom as the first of its three tenets: Not-
knowing, Bearing Witness, and Loving Action. As we let go of our
strongly held (and therefore frozen) ideas and beliefs, we can see,
hear, and know others. Thus it leads directly to witnessing life and
acting with compassion. Some call this "unknowing," and I'll
speak more of it at the end of this book. It's fundamental to all
growth.

Of course we haven't explored all the depths and all the views
on all the shores of love. Yet I hope this chapter has given you an
insight into the spiritual space that is love and a few practical open-
ers you can use to enter that space in your own lives. That is the sacred journey.

This Sack of Shit/
This Precious Human Birth

I DIDN'T MAKE UP THE TITLE
of this chapter. It comes from two Buddhist terms for the body and
the life it gives us. They symbolize two attitudes I think we all share
toward these bodies of ours. Sometimes they simply disgust us. And
sometimes we are so grateful for them.

The first phrase, "this sack of shit," comes from the Chan tradition. The pivotal Chan teacher, Linji, was fond of it, and so am I.
I mean, what is this body but a great sack of meat and mess? Linji
wrote:

> Fellow Buddhists, you drag around your begging bag
> and this sack of shit that's your body and you lose yourself
> in dead ends, looking for the Buddha, looking for the
> dharma. Right now, tell me what are you looking for in all
> your scrambling and searching?

Linji tells us to give it up, "The further you search for it, the further it recedes. Stop searching and it's right in your eyes, its sacred sound right between your ears." What the heck is he talking about? If Linji can't say, I can't say, either. But it sure sounds like this sack of shit is also the perfect Buddha body. And that's the meaning of the second term, "this precious human birth." Why is it precious? Because it allows us the chance to awaken to reality and enter nirvana.

Buddhism teaches that there are many levels of existence to be born into. They're divided into six basic realms. Lowest is the hell realm. You can imagine what that's like. You don't want to go there. Next up is the realm of hungry ghosts, sad creatures with huge stomachs and tiny little necks. They can never get enough. Some of us live our lives like hungry ghosts, don't you think? Above them are animals. We say we like them, but we don't really want to be them, do we? Above animals are us. I'll get back to us in a second. Meanwhile, above us are the *ashuras*, who are rather like the Hellenic gods or the titans. Interestingly, in some systems they're below humans, despite their powers, since they're so trapped in their passions and jealousies. Definitely above them and us are the real gods in their various heavenly worlds. Nice work if you can get it.

The really interesting thing about this cosmology, and the reason I'm telling you about it here, is this: becoming a Buddha, awakening to reality, can only happen in the human realm. Only here, among us messed-up-but-full-of-potential humans, is there the balance of suffering and delight that allows awakening. To achieve that, we need to suffer so we desire to be freed from continued rebirth, but we also need wisdom and compassion and the space to increase them. This only happens with humans. So when you think about the sheer number of other beings (especially insects, yeeccchh), you've got to realize that this human birth is truly rare and truly precious.

Since it gives us the chance to wake up, this lump of red flesh (another of Linji's names for the body) is precious and perfect, the embodiment of the Buddha and the epitome of creation. It's quite the paradox.

Hamlet (a nascent Danish bodhisattva, as we'll see farther along in this book) was also deeply torn about our bodies, saying we were "the beauty of the world! the paragon of animals! And yet, to me, what is this quintessence of dust? man delights not me; no, nor woman neither."

When he said this, Hamlet was in a notoriously bad mood, having lost all his mirth due to his uncle murdering his father and marrying his mother, so perhaps we can cut him some slack. We all have days when our dusty bodies delight us not.

This chapter is a little Buddhist instruction manual on the care and feeding of our bodies, not merely to keep us alive or even to help us find delight, but also to honor this sacred vessels that are us.

And, speaking of sacred, let's begin with that universally venerated food: pizza.

When Another Slice of Pizza Is Calling to You

Maybe for you it's a slice of cake. For me it's the lure of that last slice of pizza, still warm and lonely, waiting for me to consume its lusciousness. Whatever sings to you sings so smoothly, so sweetly, so irresistibly, your good reasons for resisting it melt away. You eat it.

Immediately you remember why you shouldn't have. You were already full, now you feel bloated and greasy. Or, perhaps worse, you feel guilty. The guilt may even have started while you were eating the thing. You couldn't even let yourself enjoy it and now, to top it off, you feel bad for it! Ugh.

This is not some situation that comes up now and then. It happens almost every day. If you can afford to buy this book, you can afford to eat too much and you probably do. To break out of this habit means breaking out of the whole cycle of desire and frustration. This is absolutely central to Buddhist practice. Pizza is a Zen teacher, constantly offering itself to you for instruction. Are you listening?

I have a hard time listening, myself. The clamor of my hunger drowns out the Sacred Voice of the Pizza. When I do hear the pizza, it's because I listen to my belly, not my brain. You can do this, too. Feel your stomach and the sensations it's sending out. Take a moment for this, just ten seconds will do. Don't clutter your head with reasons or rationalizations. Feel you stomach, then decide whether you need to eat more.

Sometimes your stomach will say "no" and you'll still eat another slice. But at least you'll be eating that last piece mindfully, aware of being in the thrall of a desire that forces you to pursue a satisfaction that neither pizza nor anything else can ever give you. But, please, give yourself some credit: the lesson itself is good and powerful. The practice of mindfulness weakens desire, even if you succumb to it.

My wife—ever my faithful and merciless critic—would like you all to note that I have never had a weight problem. While that's true, it's not quite the point. The point is always about desire and satisfaction, not weight. We become fat because we let desire overcome wisdom and satisfaction replace health. Now that is something I'm expert in, just as we all are. The lesson of mindfulness of desire applies to every single desire we have.

Here's another example of desire, one my wife will agree I'm particular susceptible to. I offer you (and me) tough love.

The Siren Song of the Snooze Button

We're busy—too busy—and we just don't sleep enough. I know how it feels to hear the alarm and succumb to the lure of the snooze button, the exquisite silence of the morning when you're still woozy from sleep, embraced in fluffy blankets and fuzzy thoughts.

But snooze buttons are an addiction, a tease, a danger. The Buddha would no doubt say something like: Using your snooze button is like shooing away a buzzing fly beneath the roar of a waterfall. The foolish person thinks the tiny noise of the fly important when all around the ground is trembling under the pounding rush of the waterfall of ignorance and desire. Let the fly buzz, wake up, and be awakened!

This is one of those "Just Say No!" situations. What does five minutes more sleep give you? Nada. Once the alarm stops your deep sleep cycle, there's no point in a few more minutes shallow rest. To grasp after those five minutes is like silencing that fly. You can do it, but the waterfall roars on. This is Buddha's fundamental teaching: giving in to desire never satisfies desire. Better to get up and use those minutes to get ahead on your day. So here's my trick:

Invest in a CD alarm clock, put a disk of music you love in it—something energetic—and set the volume pretty high. That way, instead of hearing a horrible, buzzing shriek at a quarter to six, you'll hear the nobility of Beethoven, the romance of Artie Shaw, or the energy of Nirvana. Here we are, day! Entertain us!

Cultivating the habit of realizing you're awake and using your time once that alarm goes off is a lifelong practice. Buying that CD alarm clock is the easy part. As always, start with the fundamentals.

Here is another fundamental beginning for your day—and, again another one my wife can tell you I'm still working on. This will also begin a series of solutions for the most fundamental challenge facing our bodies: finding and eating food. The whole world offers itself to us in the form of food. Receiving that offering should be a central part of our spiritual practice. We'll start with this quick solution and then go much deeper.

Grabbing a Bit of Breakfast

You've been up for half an hour and already you're running late. How did this happen? Okay, okay, just find your shoes and get out the door. No time for breakfast, just get to work! Hey, you'll save a few calories.

Does that describe your morning? It definitely describes mine. I have this unfortunate tendency to skip breakfast. Often I skip lunch too, which tends to impress everyone but my doctors and spiritual counselors. They, of course, are horrified because they know better. They know this taxes me, physically, and thus further weakens my already weak mind. What to do?

Eat breakfast.

Eating breakfast makes you smarter and can potentially burn more calories than it takes in because it speeds up your basal metabolism. When you can't eat a sit-down breakfast, eat a nutrition bar in the car or waiting for the bus. Eat it sitting down. It's easy, and these days some of those bars are actually tasty. I do it all the time when I can't force myself to eat a real breakfast.

Perhaps this doesn't sound like spiritual practice to you. Let me tell you a story. I know a guy who spent five whole years in intense and fruitless meditation and fasting. It was kind of a Hindu thing, very ascetic. Though he was a natural at meditation, he really got into fasting—eating ever smaller amounts of food until it became dangerous: one grain of rice and one bean for dinner, following that up with one tiny fruit for dessert and so on. He got so weak he couldn't break out of his spiritual rut, even though he was meditating all day. Finally, he was feeling so weak and depressed, he relented and ate breakfast. It broke his fast for real. And what happened? He was filled with the energy to immediately achieve unsurpassed supreme perfect awakening. And he did.

Okay, so that guy was Gautama Siddhartha, the Buddha, and I admit our stories are unlikely to go exactly like his did. If we're not the Buddha, eating breakfast may not lead immediately to our awakening. But in the end, spiritual energy is inseparable from physical energy, and spiritual progress cannot be made without that energy. So eat your breakfast and use that energy well. It worked for the Buddha; who are we to argue? Eating as spiritual practice— you can't beat that.

If eating can be spiritual practice, it surely can be evil or violent practice as well. In fact, all eating is violent. When you eat, you take the body of a living thing and crush it in your mouth so you can make the bits that made up its body part of your own. You can't get much more violent than that.

Some of us are torn about this. We want to minimize the harm we do to other living things, so we care about the type and number of living things we kill and eat. This inevitably raises the question of vegetarianism. The Buddha wrestled with it. I wrestle with it. I'll bet you wrestle with it. See if this helps.

If God Didn't Want Us to Eat Animals, Why Did He Make Them out of Meat?

You're torn, I know. You hate the idea of killing animals; you'd never do this intentionally. You know and despise the cold mechanization of the death factories that give us our meat today. You avoid veal because where it comes from is just too horrible. But someone's grilling a rib-eye at the barbecue, and man, does that smell good! You drool and blush simultaneously. How can you resolve this tension?

Here are two basic answers from the Buddha.

1) Feeding on anger, arrogance, deception, pride, and the like, not feeding on meat, is what makes us impure. You can't purify

your body by becoming vegetarian or even vegan. The human body is a fantastic jungle of constantly multiplying, expiring, rotting, and evolving animals. You can't change that except by dying, and even then you have to cremate yourself to finish the job. None of this matters, anyway. What matters is your mind; purify that.

2) The Buddha was not a vegetarian, and he never made monks and nuns be vegetarian, either. To this day, Theravadin monks and most Mahayana monks and nuns eat what people give them, and that includes meat.

On the other hand, there's the question of harm. We harm other creatures when we raise them, kill them, and eat them, but then we harm other creatures whatever we do. The harm we create by driving our cars is vastly greater than the harm we create by eating our burgers—and, regarding burgers, it is easy to argue that the harm we inflict on the environment and every living thing in it by raising cattle on corn is hugely greater than the harm we inflict on those cattle by killing them. If we all ate grass-fed beef instead of grain-fed beef, we'd give better lives to cattle, save the rainforest and the topsoil, and hugely improve our own health. This is why buying grass-fed beef is a good practice.

 Maybe you'd never dream of eating anything that can scream. That's excellent. Maybe bacon is your favorite food group. That's okay, too. But try to eat grass-fed beef, free-range chicken, and humanely raised pork. The Buddha would approve. No kidding.

So how does this resolve the tension of desiring meat and feeling bad about it? Put it together: it's the mind that matters, not the diet. Are you sorry

for the steak? Don't eat it. Are you hungry for it?
Dive in. You have bigger battles to fight.

Perhaps this solution sounds like an evasion to you. It isn't.
The Buddha's teaching focuses on the mind. Mind is what matters.
The bigger battle is always in your head, never on your plate. When
more suffering happens if you eat meat, end the suffering by not
eating meat. Simple. Now you're facing the bigger battle.

———

If the question of vegetarianism is the dark side of the need to eat
and the practice of eating, there ought to be a bright side as well.
There is. It's deep, it's delightful, it's fundamental. It's also grounded
and integrated by our interrelationship with all things. This fact
gives rise to respect, and that respect gives rise to a whole set of eating practices. To show their integration, I'll take us through the
process from beginning to end. . . .

Eating as a Spiritual Practice

You're hungry. You're an animal, a living organism, and to survive
you must kill and eat other living organisms. You must ingest them
and metabolize their energies, converting them to your own to keep
you alive. This is not just some cruel chemical process; you also
desire food. A hunger for it gnaws at you. When you at last get
something in that stomach, you feel satisfied, pleased, and full. This
process of hunger, desire, killing, eating, metabolizing, and satisfying happens every day. It's a jungle out there.

This process is real life. It's physically harsh and physically
wonderful. This part we know, though most of us don't think
about its life-or-death reality every day. But eating also has a spiri-

tual element, an especially Buddhist one. All that talk about desire and satisfaction? That's basic Buddhism, right there. The endless cycle of hunger, desire, and satisfaction is the endless cycle of *samsara* in a nutshell (mmmmm, nuts . . .). Put this all together and you can see how eating is a spiritual practice, or should be.

Most religious traditions have rituals to make eating more spiritual. Just think of the simple words of grace before a meal. Religious people, like monks and nuns, have many more rituals. In Buddhism they go out begging for food in the mornings, eat only from special bowls, always say certain prayers, and so on. You don't need to go that far, but there are simple things you can do to make meals a time for thanks and growth. Here are a few for different moments in the process.

Preparation

The whole world offers itself to us in the form of food. That is literally true, especially for those of us with the means to buy whatever ingredients we want from all the continents and all the seas of the world. That's quite an offering. We need to respect it.

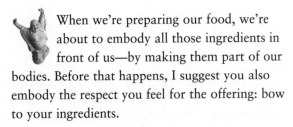 When we're preparing our food, we're about to embody all those ingredients in front of us—by making them part of our bodies. Before that happens, I suggest you also embody the respect you feel for the offering: bow to your ingredients.

This is a beautiful way to begin the process of eating. Your bow will help bring you to mindfulness of the sacrifice of other living things in the form of your food. It's not just animals; plants are alive, too, and have given themselves entirely to you. To begin the process, before you start peeling or pounding or pureeing, give your ingredients a little bow. You can do this mentally if a physical bow would disturb others. Now you're ready to lay hands on your food.

Everyone cooks. Even people who hate cooking find themselves at the grill or cutting tomatoes for a salad now and then. Those of us who cook a lot learn that touching food, and touching the ingredients that make that food, is sometimes a powerful experience and sometimes a bore. When you respect your ingredients and see their greatness, cooking is deeply rewarding. The trouble is, this rarely happens on its own.

Here's something I try when I don't spontaneously feel a deep affinity and love for the carrots or broccoli I'm cooking with. I touch each thing that was alive, thinking, "I am touching the Buddha." Think of all things as the Buddha's body. That way you're not manhandling your ingredients; you're laying hands on them. Zen teacher Dogen calls this way of touching the very process of saving all living things. When we think of things as Buddha, we elevate both them and ourselves.

If you prefer, you can think of your ingredients as the body of Christ. That's the secret of the Mass, after all: the transformation of everyday bread into the sacred body of the redeemer, offered up to feed us, body and soul. St. Ignatius, the founder of the Jesuit order, saw simple clovers and other three-part things as the Holy Trinity. For him, God was truly everywhere, sanctifying even the most humble of fields—or meals.

When you lay your hands on food this way, it ceases to be just a bunch of stuff you put in your mouth. It becomes a blessing. Note that this doesn't mean you have to slow down and get all woo-woo. Just respect its ingredients for what they are. Ask a chef: the best cooking always respects the ingredients. The practice is not just spiritual, it's tasty, and that applies to the simplest chow as well as the most refined meal. I can testify that the greatest meals I've ever had have always involved sincere respect for their ingredients.

Presentation

When you're done with preparation, you're ready for presentation. This can be brief, and in fact I think it should be brief. I'm not a fan of tricking out food to look super-elegant—or, even worse, to look like something it's not.

I encourage you to let your food be what it is and let those who are going to eat it see what it is. Present your food so everyone can appreciate the sacrifice and the celebration it represents. This continues the process of respect you began with that first bow to your ingredients.

Serving

Now we are about ready to eat, but of course one thing needs to come first. Grace.

Perhaps you think of grace as a Christian thing. You're right; it is a Christian thing. It's also a Jewish thing, a Muslim thing, a Hindu thing, a Jain thing, a Confucian, Taoist, Sikh, Zoroastrian,

Native American, shamanic, and Buddhist thing. It's all these things because all religious traditions recognize the beauty—the sacredness—of gratitude for a meal.

If you want some Buddhist inspiration, here is something Zen groups say:

> *Now we praise the Three Treasures*
> *and are grateful for this meal.*
> *Innumerable labors bring it to us,*
> *the gift of other living beings.*

Isn't that lovely? You can make it even shorter, saying "Innumerable labors bring us this food, the gift of other living beings." Another chant begins, "Innumerable labors brought us this food. We should know how it comes to us." Ah, but that is complex! Food comes through the labors of weeders and pickers, from planters before them and drivers after, from the thousand bees who pollinate the flowers and the million earthworms who enrich the soil, and from the innocent, growing, living things that make themselves a gift to us. We're all bound together in food, a circle as wide as life. There it is, on your table. All those energies are not dead; wondrously they bring life to you. Say a word of praise!

In your own praise at serving, you can make something up or use the tried and true words of others. You can vary your thoughts or make one phrase your constant blessing. You can speak in your heart or share your words with all at your table. The world is always present and always listening.

Eating

Now we come to it: taking the gift of life inside you. Bring your mind along.

If all has gone well so far, you feel desire for your food. This is dukkha; this is the nature of life. But you're lucky: this particular desire is being satisfied. Be here for the big show! Your desire is okay. Your satisfaction is okay. Place your attention inside. Stop watching the damn TV! A sandwich is pleasure enough. And your pleasure is yet another form of respect for your food. Have it.

There, that was an easy one, wasn't it?

Cleaning Up

All things must pass. And then they must get put away. Help things find their way to their resting places.

Cleaning up is purifying. It is creating order. It is making a little corner of the world right and good. Cleaning up after dinner is making your kitchen right and good. I know this can seem dull.

Bring cleaning to life by making it your final offering of thanks to all those beings who did all those labors to bring you your meal. Pick up the dishes from the table, carrying them gently. Save leftovers grateful for their patience as they wait to give themselves again. Scrape off the plates with gratitude. Load the dishwasher or do the dishes mindful of the water. And, putting away, let yourself take pleasure in the perfection of things in their places. All these actions can be empowering if you simply see their essences.

The whole process of preparing, presenting, thanking, eating, and cleaning is truly a place for powerful practice, sadly neglected by most spiritual followers. We commonly consider eating a shallow practice. Perhaps, perhaps. Yet we do it every day. We may go weeks without finding time to meditate, but we always find time to eat. Make eating a meditation and you make it a fundamental practice on your path.

Now I want to move beyond eating to the results of eating: our healthy and sometimes voluptuous bodies. In most post-industrial countries, we're trained to disparage oversized bodies, and, when they are our own, to try to change them. I want to suggest another way to see them.

Beautifully Rounded Buddha, Beautifully Rounded You

When you imagine a statue of the Buddha, what do you imagine? What does the Buddha look like? You go to a museum and see the statues, or, better yet, you just go to your local Chinese restaurant. There's a statue there and that guy looks very round and very happy. Or perhaps it's a graceful woman, smiling slightly, standing in her elegant robes. But look at her face; she's no waif, is she?

That's right: Buddha images all over the world are never skinny. They're always relaxed, including their waistlines. Some of them are of Shakyamuni, the historical Buddha; some are of incarnations of Manjushri, the bodhisattva of wisdom; some are of Guanyin or Avalokiteshvara, the bodhisattva of compassion. None of them is worrying about weight.

> Well, there is one kind of Buddha images that does show Gautama Siddhartha worrying about his weight. He's so worried he's fasting, and he's skinny as a rail. In fact, he's barely more than a skeleton and on the verge of death. He looks it, too. What is crucial to note here is that these statues are of Siddhartha *before* he became a Buddha. As soon as he stopped fasting, he got awakened. These statues are the anti-role model for Buddhist bodies.

We, on the other hand, are constantly worrying about our weight, even when it's not about health but simply about vanity. For instance, when I was young, my parents always wanted me to put on five pounds, in case I got sick. Well, I've done it now and it's bugging me ridiculously. Makes me want to get sick just to lose the weight. That is not sensible—and I'm a mild case. People who are socialized to base their self-worth on their sexual attractiveness can really collapse when they believe they are fat and not beautiful.

So, when you feel upset about your weight, visualize yourself as the Buddha or a great celestial bodhisattva. Shut your eyes; relax your breathing; just let it happen. Follow your breaths and, as you do, visualize looking down at your body as this beautiful—and beautifully rounded—being. It's okay, in fact it's holy and wonderful, to be this being: soft, pliant, ample, radiant. Let that feel good. It *is* good. When you're ready, open your eyes and be yourself. You may not look much like the Buddha. In fact perhaps your only real similarity is being ample. An excellent start.

It makes perfect sense that Buddhism recommends being in the middle regarding weight: not too skinny, not too fat. After all, Buddhism isn't called the Middle Path for nothing. You can think of this path as reflecting the Buddha's own hard-won realization that extremes of self-indulgence (his first 25 years) and self-denial (his next five years) just don't help. They don't bring happiness. For 2500 years, Buddhism has promoted an intelligently flexible way of moving forward along a path while avoiding the extremes.

We've been talking about food for long enough to give you plenty to consider on your own. Now it's time to take a look at other desires and other practices. One practice that most religions have worked with and been conflicted about is drinking alcohol or ingesting some other substance that alters the mind. Again, it shouldn't surprise you that the Buddha and I chart a middle path on drugs.

Getting Really Drunk

The high we feel on alcohol or marijuana or harder drugs allures us. Why? Because it alters our state; it breaks us "out of our mind"; it releases us from the prison of our personality. It's not mere chance that "personality" comes from the Greek word for "mask." It's you, but if it's the only mask you have, then it's a role, a trap. No one wants to be trapped. Getting high frees you.

Or does it? Buddhism does not forbid getting drunk or high. But the first precept of Buddhism, the first principle to try to follow, is to avoid harming our minds and bodies with intoxicants. Here's the rule of thumb:

 1) Before you drink, smoke, drop, shoot up, or whatever, ask "Will this ruin my awareness?" If so, then don't do it. If not, then go to number two. . . .

2) While you're drunk/high/whatever, ask "Have I lost my awareness, my insight?" If the answer is no, then simply remain aware of yourself as you continue your experience. If yes, then you've broken the precept, and you need to devote yourself to awareness of your lack of awareness as you come down.

You can be "really" drunk. Being "really" drunk (or stoned or whatever) is being newly aware of something real in yourself, something revealed by this new state. Taking off your mask can teach you and others a lot about you. When this happens, don't condemn, don't congratulate. Just look at yourself. Can you respect this person? Do you like this person? Who is this person? Is this person you?

If you ask yourself "Have I lost my awareness, my insight?" and the answer is yes, then you're not "really" drunk. You're just wasted. You're not free, you're trapped in the drug. This harms you. Still, don't condemn yourself; just go home.

Tricky stuff, answering those questions about awareness on drugs. On the other hand, try asking the same basic question, right now: Am I aware? I don't know about you, but there is no end to what I'm not aware of, even in myself, right now. Part of the problem is the limited power of our brains. We like to think they can comprehend the universe, but they're really just a bit too small in the end. Nevertheless, we can train them, and we need to.

Your Brain: Use It or Lose It

I'm only half-joking in this scenario's title. In fact you're not going to lose your brain if you don't exercise it. Parts of your brain are always working, whether you're conscious of it, or not. Those parts will keep on working until you die, thank goodness.

That's nice, but what about the parts of your brain you are conscious of? Does the old exercise mantra of "use it or lose it" apply to them? Not to be too blunt about it, but *yes*.

Some encouraging studies have shown that education at any time in life, and continuing mental exercise (even fun stuff like reading books, doing crossword puzzles or playing complex card games) as we age, can strongly protect us against Alzheimer's (and this is true even if we *get* it). Some really stark studies have also shown the opposite: that many folks like college professors die or get Alzheimer's soon after they retire unless they replace their teaching brain work with some other kind of brain work. It doesn't matter what kind, it just needs to be something that pumps up the brain. We're all like this, in our own way, so if we don't want Alzheimer's we're wise to give our brains a workout now and then.

So, what's the trick? May I suggest: Just add Buddha. Literally, read a book on the Buddha. Ah, you already are; excellent! But this book is too easy. Try working through a long text like the *Lotus Sutra* or the *Bodhicharyavatara*. Or how about picking up bridge? Or a weekly poker game? Or a musical instrument? Or a new language? Crossword puzzles in French? *Tout est bon.* It's all good. Just make sure you turn off the TV.

The stories tell us the Buddha stayed sharp until the very moment of his death at age 80, which was exceptionally old back then. He did this by eating a healthy diet, going on regular walks, and always teaching the dharma, learning new insights and developing new techniques throughout his long teaching career. Let's strive to emulate the Buddha in all these ways.

How wrong can you go, emulating the Buddha? Healthy diet, healthy exercise, healthy mind. He was the definition of *mens sana in corpore sano*: a healthy mind in a healthy body.

This next scenario, depression, is something that bridges the *mens* and the *corpore*. Naturally, the solution bridges them, too.

Treating Depression (with Respect and Sweat)

You're depressed. We all get this way. Everything seems like work. Even supposedly fun things don't seem worth the effort. Why fix a big dinner when you don't really care what you're eating? Why fix dinner when you're not really hungry? Why even eat at all? Isn't it just an endless cycle leading to one thing: death?

Well, yes. Congratulations, your depression is dukkha. Your realizing this is an absolutely vital spiritual insight. It is natural and right and logical. Give yourself credit. That's the first step: immediately stop criticizing yourself for being depressed. Accept this depression as part of the whole world of cause and effect. You're depressed for reasons philosophical, personal, and chemical. This is not a failure. It's just depression.

Now take the next step in cause and effect: create a cause that will help lead to breaking your depression. Mind is what matters in Buddhism, as the Buddha and I never tire of reminding you (and ourselves). Your mind is a complex set of processes that you can control more than you might imagine. Anti-depressant drugs are one way to cause your depression to break. Taking them helps creates that cause. You also have nonchemical ways. Here's one very simple practice.

When you're depressed, exercise. Exercise is proven to change your body chemistry, including the chemistry in your brain, so if you wake up depressed and just don't feel you can tackle the day, take fifteen minutes and go running. If you can't do that, run up your stairs for fifteen minutes (but please walk back down; running down stairs is bad for your joints even if you don't fall). Do knee bends or jumping jacks or walk with a backpack or a dog who's happy to push the pace. The action doesn't matter, just make sure there's some action and your heart gets pumping. Do this a.s.a.p. If you're depressed at work, get a nutrition bar instead of a full lunch so you'll have time to go for a brisk walk. You can get your heart rate up without getting too sweaty. Sweat is optional; heartbeats are not. Don't expect to have fun, just do it.

Depression can be serious business. The simple solution of exercise is for those of us who have an average expectable depression coming from an average expectable life. Those who suffer from serious clinical depression are going to need more help. Still, exercise should be part of their lives and their therapies as well.

Let your body re-create your brain. Your brain will re-create your mind. And your mind will re-create your future.

Body, brain, mind—in the final analysis they are simply not separable. They illustrate the central Buddhist idea of dependent co-origination, or, as Thich Nhat Hanh phrases it, interbeing. All things "inter-are" because no things exist apart from all other things. Even apparently separate things like, say, George W. Bush and Osama bin Laden are in fact not separate. They constantly create each other (and not just politically, either). How much more so with our bodies, brains, and minds? In constant change and reciprocal interbeing, our personal world of body, brain, and mind evolves.

This knowledge is not just something interesting. We can use it. For instance, we can use it to empower us when the physical aspect of our environment seems unpleasant.

Sweating Your Brains Out/
Freezing Your Butt Off

There's nothing worse than being stuck in a sweltering building in the middle of summer when every wall seems hotly menacing and the humidity is as high as your head. Or maybe there *is* something worse: those times when you're waiting for your ride—who's late because of the snow—and the only thing that's distracting you from imagining your little toes have surely frozen and turned black is the unbelievably crushing ache your earlobes insist on sharing with the inside of your skull.

Ah, but in fact, nasty as those situations are, not only are there many worse things than them, those sensations of heat and cold are in no way intrinsically bad. We are trained by our bodies and our cultures to dislike feeling hot or cold, but we can unlearn this training. That goes for minor pain, as well. Such feelings, like so much in life, are changeable through acceptance.

Anthropologists studying especially rugged cultures and those who have observed wild children raised outside society have claimed that these unusual people really don't feel heat and cold the way we do. Their experience of being out in the elements only approaches real discomfort when it is physically dangerous. They skipped the training we all got that made us so sensitive to such minor changes in temperature.

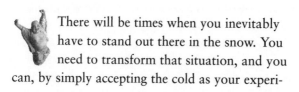 There will be times when you inevitably have to stand out there in the snow. You need to transform that situation, and you can, by simply accepting the cold as your experi-

ence rather than rebelling against it. Fighting the cold by opposing it just doesn't work. Instead, fight it by accepting it as okay with you. It is simply a certain type of neurological stimulus. This practice works in all but extreme and dangerous situations, which is good, because extreme pain from heat or cold or injury is about alerting us to quickly end the situation causing it. It doesn't take the Buddha to teach you to do that! Where you need the Buddha is to remind you that minor pain or heat or cold is part of life that cannot be ended but doesn't have to be dukkha. It's not bad unless you say it is. Let go of the "bad" and start training yourself to accept what is without labels.

There's a well-known Zen koan dealing with exactly this issue of perceiving heat and cold.

> *A monk asked, "What does it mean to go where there's no cold and no heat?" Teacher Dongshan said, "In the cold, cold freezes you; in the heat, heat burns you up."*

> Blue Cliff Record 43

Of course, the koan, being a teaching story and religious practice designed to lead the student to deeper awakening, is about much more than the physical situation of cold and heat. It's about awakening itself, the not-two-ness of reality, and so on. Dongshan was a great teacher. In fact, his very name has been incorporated into the largest Zen school in Japan: Soto Zen (he's the "to" in Soto). It's no wonder he can speak simultaneously of the air temperature, the body, and the ecstasy of awakening. But that's deep stuff, and we're talking about the fundamentals. On the most basic level, we can at least see how the koan ties right into our trick: let the cold and heat do their thing. There's no problem until we make one.

We are moving along nicely. We've covered food and weight, we've talked about exercise (both mental and physical), and we've discussed making the mind a better place for us to be, with no problems until we make them. What have we missed?

Ah yes, we haven't dealt with the way we all got here in the first place: sex. In Chapter Three I wrote about deepening sex. That's important, but what about the wisdom of having sex in the first place? I've saved that question until now because it's not so much about love as it is about the body itself and what to do with it. It's an intensely physical and literally vital thing to ask. . .

Is It Okay to Have Sex Now?

That is an important question. Not asking it has caused a whole lot of people pain, from primitives to postmoderns, from paupers to presidents. There is simply no separating physical acts of sex from their emotional, moral, legal, and spiritual results. So, let's say you're in a situation where the question might come up (so to speak). I won't describe the scenario for you here—this is a book for adults, but it's not an "adult book." I think you can imagine situations where the question is a tough one. What to do? Here's a quick set of questions borrowed from Judie O'Neill's and Bridget Fonger's very wise and practical book, *The Lazy Woman's Guide to Just About Everything*.

Who—someone you trust?
What—an act you are comfortable with?
Where—a safe place?
Why—a healthy, non-compulsive reason?
How—Are you practicing safe sex?

Now that is some refreshingly useful advice that takes only second to put into practice. Just ask the questions. You should ask them before the actual sex is happening, of course.

Ask and answer. Get right to the facts. You're like a reporter covering your own story. You want just the straight answers: who, what, where, why, and how. If those answers are not the positive ones O'Neill and Fonger point to, then stop. There's no complexity and there's no excuse. Just stop.

This is one of those solutions I sometimes offer that don't sound very Buddhist—but are. To ask such questions is to open yourself to insight. Looking inside for the answers is mindfulness practice. Did you think that mindfulness was only of spiritual things? It isn't. It's mindfulness about—duh—what's in your mind. If you're about to have sex, then what's in your mind are thoughts of sex and sensations of attraction and arousal, and, we hope, awareness of the other person and the surroundings and your relationship and protection from pregnancy, STDs, and so on. Mindfulness leads not only to deeper awareness of what is, it also leads to better choices of what to do.

It's remarkable how practical and down-to-earth Buddhism is. That's one of the many reasons I and millions of other people love

Buddhism. Walking a Buddhist path means being aware, informed, responsive, positive, and skillful. "Skillful" is a particularly Buddhist word. The Buddha taught us to be skillful inside and out. Choosing to have sex when the situation is right is being skillful on the outside. That sort of thing can be tough, but it's easier than being skillful on the inside. As I said about vegetarianism, the real battle is always in our minds. There is where skillful thought and action begin.

The mind is also where unskillful thought and action begin. We'll cover much of that ground in the next chapter (as if you couldn't guess from its title). I want to end this chapter with one solution for a problem that bridges it and the next: anxiety. Anxiety is nearly always experienced as physical as well as mental. It gnaws at the body as well as the mind. It's entirely unpleasant, but it's entirely self-produced. Why do we go there, and how do we get back?

A Buddhist Prescription for Anxiety

Perhaps, like me, you sometimes lie awake at night anxious about an upcoming conference or speech or new course you're teaching. You can lie there spinning this huge ball of fear around in your stomach until it actually becomes a physical pain. This used to happen to me when I was a kid. From my anxiety I'd create a real pain, sharp and insistent. It may have been psychosomatic, but it sure hurt, and once I got it, making it go away was so hard I was trapped in my anxiety and wasn't even sure why I was so anxious. The cycle feeds on itself.

We need to distinguish such anxieties from specific concerns. Concerns are concrete issues you can work on. Anxieties are free-floating feelings you can't do anything about, only experience. Buddha says give it up! Spending time dwelling on anxieties is useless because it does not help you minimize your dukkha. In fact, it perpetuates dukkha because it distracts your attention and energy from things you can actually change.

You can take the first step toward giving up the useless practice of anxiety this way. First, notice how your anxiety is spinning wheels without getting traction. Anxiety doesn't clarify any concrete actions you can take to reduce the anxiety. If you've been feeling anxious about something for ten minutes and you haven't come up with an action that might help, say this (preferably out loud): "I'm sick of thinking about this. Instead of anxiety, here are three possible actions." Then just speak those three actions. They can be totally dumb or impossible or funny or evil. Doesn't matter. Just say them.

From this first step, two things arise. First, you immediately short circuit your emotional spinning. This is true especially if you've imagined a possible action that's way out of character. Second, you'll immediately begin imagining more realistic scenarios that move you forward in your thought. As long as you're thinking this way, you don't have anxiety; you have concerns. And you're not stewing in them; you're working on them.

From the perspective of Buddhism, we can see this as an example of changing a mental state from unskillful to skillful (*akusala* to *kusala*, in case you want to know the Pali terms). An unskillful state is one in which the cause not controlled and the effect is unpleasant. Letting ourselves be anxious is focusing on the effect. That's unskillful. We can't control effects, only causes, so what matters here is controlling the cause, changing it to one that doesn't produce unpleasant feelings. Looking into possible actions is focusing on the cause and what to do about it. That's skillful.

As with most changes to skillful action, this skillful refocusing on actions doesn't mean you'll find the perfect action right away; it takes time and effort to do so. This *does* mean you'll skillfully change your mind and experience. That happens right away as you replace anxiety with imagination.

Here's another trick, a traditional way of reconceiving problems in the Tibetan tradition. If a problem can be solved, there is no need to worry about it. And if it cannot be solved, then there is also no reason to worry about it. This is true because, if it can be solved, all you need is enough effort and you'll solve it. No worries. Conversely, if it cannot be solved, then no effort can accomplish it and no anxiety can help it. No worries. This little gem, like so many others, comes from Shantideva's *Bodhicharyavatara*.

Hmmm, "replacing anxiety with imagination," that about sums up the whole path of Buddhism and, for that matter, the whole path to happiness. Changing mental states from unhappy to happy, from *dukkha* to *sukkha*. That's what the Buddha taught and that's what I'm teaching in this book. Now we're really focusing on the mind, the unending task of setting it straight. You've done a lot, already. Why not take a breather—literally, enjoy your breathing. Then, when you're ready, turn to the next chapter, where we'll jump into your brain.

5

It's All in Your Mind

REFRESHED AND REJUVE-
nated, we're ready to dive into the gray matter of the mind (which
is different from diving into the gray matter of the brain—gross).
As with all complex and vital things, the mind is not all good or all
bad. It's a gray area where practice never quite makes perfect. Still,
practice does make the mind better, a good mind makes life better,
and a good life makes the world better. So, let's see what we can do
to work on the mind, where it all begins.

In this chapter, I present a range of situations and solutions aris-
ing in states of mind. Their origins in the mind hold them together.
And, as their origins lie inside, so do their solutions. Let's begin with
one that doesn't merely begin strictly inside, but remains there.

Capturing a Dream

You're dreaming and on the edge of some vital insight. Or you're
in touch with a powerful desire. Or you're afraid of something and
starting to realize what it is. Then you wake up.

That happens to all of us. Dreams blow away in the wind of waking. It's unavoidable, since these two states of consciousness, dreaming and waking, are incompatible. Yet dreams can teach us if we let them. Several schools of Buddhism have systems of cultivating and analyzing dreams. After all, in Buddhism the normal state of consciousness we call "waking" is itself something to be awakened from. If we can learn from this dream we call life, we can surely learn from the dreams we call dreams.

 When you wake and feel a sense of groping for a lost dream, let yourself drift. Do not strive to remember consciously. Let yourself drift back to the physical or emotional sense of the dream and see what comes up in your mind. Not only is this a relaxed and mindful way to begin your day, you can learn things about yourself you only reveal in dreams.

One more thing—and I guarantee this is wonderfully practical advice: do not share your dreams. This not because they lose their spiritual power if you do; it is because they are so boring to everyone else in the world. If someone insists on hearing them, you may indulge, but do not try this with any but most gracious listeners.

Dreams stay in our heads (unless we divulge them), yet they also influence our lives. That's because they are not only shaped by who we are; they also *shape* who we are. We work through problems in dreams, and we're well advised to pay attention to what we experience there.

We pay attention to dreams, both while we have them and afterward, to learn from our inner fantasies. We learn about ourselves and about how better to fit ourselves into our lives. But we fantasize in waking life, as well, and we can harness those fantasies.

When You Can't Stop Thinking about Something

We often get caught up in obsessing about something that's about to happen. It might be as simple as whether our team will win the big game, or as important as whether our candidate will win the big election. It might be something we can barely influence, like these examples, or it might be something we powerfully control, like how our date will go on Saturday night. Whatever it is, however vital it might be, if it takes you away from living in this present moment, let it go.

I learned from renowned psychiatrist Mardi Horowitz, M.D., a wonderful way of dealing with fantasies—a way that has much to do with Buddhism. Here's what Dr. Horowitz suggests: take a minute to fantasize about the best-case scenario for the situation, where everything you could hope for comes true. Enjoy that. Then think of the worst-case scenario, where everything you fear in this situation comes to pass. Experience that. Next, appreciate what you've done: you've seen how you get through it

either way, no matter what. You are ready for
what comes.

This is wise and empowering advice. When you replace vague hopes or fears with realistic ones, you bring an unapproachable problem down to approachable size. You find that on a practical level, you can cope. Underneath this practical technique is a Buddhist truth—in fact, you might say, *the* Buddhist truth: following the middle way. Buddhism, the religion, begins with the Buddha's very first teaching, to his five old companions in the forest. In that first lesson, the Buddha taught the middle way, the path between the two extremes of self-indulgence and self-denial. Buddhists have been walking that path ever since.

When you obsess on the future, you can snap out of it by imagining the two extremes: one where you are fully indulged, one where you are totally denied. Seeing those, you'll realize neither of those is really going to happen; what will happen is something in the middle. Opening your eyes to the middle way of real life will in turn help you open yourself to the middle way of Buddhism.

Once again, the solution comes down to opening yourself to reality.

The following scenario and solution don't fit quite neatly into any one aspect of the Eightfold Path, but they certainly happen, and the solution sure helps.

Written by a Man Slowly Being Driven Insane by His Neighbor's Dog

They say that for the awakened, all the sounds of the world are the sound of the Buddha's voice. Well that's just great for them, isn't it?

They're already awakened, and as if that weren't good enough, they hear all sounds as pure and beautiful, the bastards! So I ask, what about the rest of us, huh? What about that howling dog? My neighbor's dog has been howling at night for five years, since he was just a puppy. The wretched thing is still howling now! Once he opens his mouth, the sound just streams out, wailing, angry, and desperate. This is not the kind of awakening I was hoping for.

My practice, then, is to turn those pitiful howls into the pleasing sound of the dharma. And of course, the howls' pitifulness is where I find the solution I want to share with you. That poor dog is so unhappy! His little world is so unsatisfying. He cries out, and I hear him. When I think of our relationship, I think of Kanzeon, the great bodhisattva "who hears the cries of the world." I think of myself as Kanzeon. Talk about empowering!

Try this yourself when your neighbors are fighting or cheering, or the party down the block is busting out, or even when the helicopters sound as mad as the dogs. When you hear the shouts and howls around you, imagine yourself as Kanzeon, who hears the cries of the world. You are to the howling dog as Kanzeon is to you: a being of enormous compassion and inconceivable powers. Hear those cries in pity. Think of Kanzeon inside you to give you patience. Cry out to Kanzeon, and you can bear the listening you have to do yourself.

I'm calling this celestial bodhisattva "Kanzeon," the Japanese version of the name that best translates as "the one who hears the cries of the world." Kanzeon is just one name of many for this central Buddhist figure, the embodiment of compassion, which along with wisdom comprise the central Buddhist virtues. In the original Sanskrit, the name is Avalokiteshvara; in Chinese, Guanyin; in Korean, Kwanum; in Vietnamese, Quan Am; in Tibetan, Chenrezig. The bod-hisattva of compassion will exist, taking the form of many beings, as long as there are living things to save. For instance, Vajrayana Buddhists believe he is presently embod-ied as the Dalai Lama. He does look awful compassionate, you must admit. Yet, in East Asia, Guanyin looks quite femi-nine and is even sometimes referred to as "she," not "he." Wherever he's called, whoever invokes her, Guanyin is surely the most beloved bodhisattva in all Buddhism.

What do you think, does this scenario fit into right view? Right intention? Right action? Right effort? Perhaps all of them, in some way? I incline to that last answer. The middle path has eight aspects, not eight divisions. The path is integral, and though it is helpful to concentrate on one or another aspect of it to learn and to practice, in the end the path remains one. As Thich Nhat Hanh might say, each aspect "inter-is."

Here is a scenario that illumines another aspect of inter-being. It is true that the mind leads the world and all things must follow. It is also true that no man is an island. When things are going poorly in the mind, it is wise to remember this truth and even to use it.

When You're Discouraged and Don't See How to Cheer Yourself Up

There are plenty of times when I get down. Maybe I'm behind on a deadline or disappointed at not getting something I've worked hard for. Or maybe I'm just plain grumpy. Buddhist authors can be grumpy too, damn it!

We all get this way, sometimes, and when we do, the lower we get, the less power we feel to snap ourselves out of it. Our discouragement dissuades us from encouraging ourselves. Luckily, there is a way out of this circular trap.

 When you're feeling discouraged, blast out of it by helping someone else. You can lose *your* troubles by losing yourself in someone *else's* troubles. There's nothing like seeing another person's dukkha to make you forget your own for a time. This works even better when you actually help get rid of the other person's dukkha. Get up, go to someone else's cubicle, and offer them help. Or go online and answer someone's question. There are always a hundred people out there in the world around you and in cyberspace who need your knowledge and whom you can make happy, if you can just connect up with them. Or fix someone a snack. When was the last time a snack someone else made for you didn't cheer you up fix one for them, you'll see the difference it makes. For that time, your troubles are over.

What you do doesn't matter, so do the first thing that offers it-self or comes to mind. I can't give you specifics; they will arise from whatever situation you're in. Look around you. Who's there? What do they need help with? Go help them with it.

Do you know why this works to make you feel better? Do you know what you are when you act this way?

You are a bodhisattva. I bow to you.

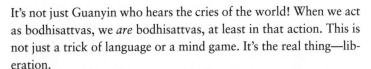

It's not just Guanyin who hears the cries of the world! When we act as bodhisattvas, we *are* bodhisattvas, at least in that action. This is not just a trick of language or a mind game. It's the real thing—lib-eration.

Zen teacher Taigen Dan Leighton Sensei, who I've mentioned before, has written a truly beautiful book on just this subject, called *Faces of Compassion*. In it, he introduces us to the major bod-hisattvas and how they act in the world. He doesn't stop there, though. He goes on to give examples of present day people who embody those bodhisattva attributes. I just mentioned the Dalai Lama as the bodhisattva of compassion. That's classic, but how about Mother Teresa as well? Albert Einstein as Manjushri, the bodhisattva of wisdom? Mahatma Gandhi as Samantabhadra, the bodhisattva of awakened action? How about you as Vimalakirti, the great exemplar of the lay person? Fire yourself up, go get Leighton's book.

In fact, it's not only bodhisattvas that we can be when we act like it: we can be Buddhas. Zen Teacher Dogen expressed this bet-ter than anyone (well, better than anyone but the Buddha who ex-pressed it by being . . . uh . . . the Buddha):

*When Buddhas are really Buddhas they may not
even notice they're Buddhas. Still, they are manifested
Buddhas who continue to manifest Buddhas.*

Genjo Koan 2

*There's a simple way to become Buddha: avoid
unskillful activity, detach from life and death, feel
compassion for all living things, respect superiors
and help inferiors, end your aversions and desires,
and go without schemes and worries. Then, you'll be
named Buddha. Do not seek anything else.*

Birth and Death 5

There you have it. It's simple to be a Buddha. Right. In fact, I
agree it's simple to be a Buddha, but *becoming* a Buddha is brain-
bogglingly hard. Perhaps even becoming a Buddha is simple, but
simple does not mean easy, not by a long shot. Still, the Buddha
taught humans because we are teachable; we're not lost causes. It's
true that the myths say he didn't want to teach us at first. He
thought it would be too hard and a waste of time. Luckily the gods
intervened and convinced him to try anyway, for their sake as well
as ours. Gods need awakening too. The Buddha relented, and
Dogen testifies that the system works. Now if we could just manage that bit about going without schemes and worries. . . .

Those Sad Words:
"I Could Have" and "If Only"

I should have . . . I could have . . . If only . . .

So sad, and yet how we dwell on them! We replay our failures
and even other people's failures that matter to us. It's another vi-

cious circle we need to snap out of. Here's a non-threatening example. I experience "if only" regarding Game Six of the 2002 World Series, when the Giants, my team, blew a five-run lead in the eighth inning—the largest, latest lead ever blown by a baseball team about to become champions. This is a really first class "if only" opportunity. (Of course I admit that Cubs and Red Sox fans have many more.) I realize the stakes are pretty low here, but the dynamic is very clear. I dwell on this failure. I replay it in my head: Why, oh why, did Dusty take out Russ Ortiz so quickly? Why did Felix Rodriguez throw so many fastballs in a row to Scott Spiezio? These questions continue while the miserable images play over and over in my mind. I'm trapped in the reality of this failure, re-experiencing it in my memory.

 The solution is to separate the reality from the re-experiencing. Whatever it was that you're trapped in, ask yourself: Wasn't it bad enough the first time? Really ask, and really answer. If your answer is "yes," then drop the miserable thing. No reason to hold onto it. Asking the question will help you let go. Don't stick with the pain you've got, simply because it's real and it's yours. The Buddha is not cool with that. Move on. If you're like me, sometimes you'll even laugh at yourself. The Buddha is definitely cool with that.

But maybe your answer to "Wasn't it bad enough the first time?" is "Well. . . ." In this case, the experience still has something to teach you. You need to move on to the learning phase. For example, I can use my World Series "if only" opportunity as a chance to feel petty, sad, and embittered. Or I can choose to use it to look into my desire and attachment to suffering in an almost comical way. Well, okay, it's not "almost" comical, it *is* comical, but it's also serious. We can more easily learn from these little miseries; we can then apply the knowledge to the big ones. We have these opportunities constantly. Sports provide them. Our reactions to TV shows provide them. Even second-guessing fictional characters can teach us about ourselves. That's why the Buddha and Jesus taught in parables. Use episodes from your own life as parables. You have much to teach yourself.

It's remarkable how we can not only worry about our future; we can worry about our past. We are definitely not following Dogen's advice when we do the "if only" thing, yet at least we can learn from ourselves when we do. Eventually, such scheming and worrying falls away completely. Or so they tell me.

Since we're discussing negative mindsets and unskillful mental indulgences, let's confront the greatest of all: anger. Yes, we love to indulge in anger. It makes us feel good, even as it makes us feel bad. On balance—and when we're not angry—we admit this is not a wise choice, but that doesn't stop us from falling right into it again at the first opportunity. Why on earth do we do this? And how can we stop ourselves?

What Feeds Anger? Anger

It's true on the biggest scale: the politics of rage and hatred in the Middle East. It's true on the smallest scale: the grumbling frustration we have at our own persistent faults. And it's true in between: the ongoing anger we have with our personal friends and enemies as we have to live with and around them. What is this thing that is always true? That anger breeds anger. Anger is the fuel for further anger, somehow feeding on itself and growing as we give it greater energy.

Both Western psychological research and Buddhism tell us the same thing, basing their views on both rigorous empirical testing and deep spiritual insight. There's simply no denying it. Holding onto anger, even if we are righteous and morally correct, just does no good. Expressing anger creates conditions—karmic and physiological—that make one more susceptible to anger. Expressing anger is a form of practice, in this case practicing the ability to be angry. Does that sound smart to you? I thought not.

There are rare times when clearing out anger may be good. You might decide to pummel a pillow, for example. I've done this and immediately felt better. But then the real practice begins: letting go of long-term anger and cultivating patience and tolerance in its place. So think of this practice as two-phased:

1) Release you anger quickly—never at a living target, of course. Pummel the pillow, whack the wall hangings, assault the ottoman, whatever releases the physical wave of anger. I find that very loud swearing helps, as well. (Aren't I saintly?) Really get it out so you won't return to the same emotion about the same issue. Banish your anger as you release it.

2) Keep the release going by shifting to the ongoing practice of replacing it permanently with its inverse. Retrain your mind. If I could give you a quick solution for retraining your mind, I

would, but the fact is you've been training yourself to hold onto anger for decades. Retraining takes time. One tip is to let yourself enjoy the relaxation you feel when you consciously make this choice. Say you're having a spat with your boss. You feel anger from him and you feel anger in you. You choose to ignore your anger, leaving it on its own to get lonely and crawl off somewhere. Feel the inner spaciousness this gives you. It's your first reward. Others will come much later. In the meantime, let yourself enjoy this one.

In changing from unskillful to skillful mind states, we change from living in one small place to living simultaneously in two places. We live in the small self, the one that may or may not be skillful at any given moment. We also, increasingly, live in the large self, which really is no self at all. It is the freedom that lies beyond the self and selfishness. This shift takes a long time, perhaps longer than a lifetime, yet you can begin it every moment.

Performance Anxiety

Are you taking a driving test? You're nervous. Are you about to ask someone out? You're nervous. Do you have to present something at work? You're nervous. Of course you are. When you care about the result and focus on yourself in the situation, you notice that you're nervous. There is nothing wrong with this.

The trouble comes when you let your focus on you pull you away from the real world. Then it's not about the driving test anymore; it's about your fumbling with the gearshift and forgetting what's the order for looking in the rearview mirror and the side mirror. Then it's not about the person you're asking out; it's about becoming hyper-aware of the sound of your voice, or how your pants are too short, or whether your sweat is showing on your shirt. When you're in this kind of loop, you've stepped in your own way. You've got to butt out.

Your anxiety is exactly that: yours. Forget about yourself and you forget about your anxiety. There's no one to have it. We can never do this completely, but we can make a huge leap by simply changing our mental focus. For example, when I'm anxious about speaking in public, I let go of my self and remember that talking is all about you (or whomever I'm talking to). Then I lose my fear. I lose it because I lose my sense of self. It's a liberation. Anxiety gets replaced by energy and conviction. Now I'm free to teach the dharma as much as I understand it, even if that's just a little.

Get your focus back on real life. The solution is to replace your thoughts of you with thoughts of life. I know, I know; not easy. But one trick lies in what I just said: replace your thoughts. When you try not to think about something, it automatically comes up. You can't just take thoughts away; you need to replace them. When your negative thoughts are anxious ones, the obvious way to replace them is with thoughts of the thing you care about. You plainly care about this thing or you wouldn't be anxious. So when you feel anxiety, focus your thoughts on what you care about, enjoy, and love. Cease thinking of yourself and your role. Think only of what is good in the matter at hand. When your thoughts stray back toward anxiety, focus even more tightly on what you care about: the smell of home; the night you first kissed; the front door of your dream home; that charming, unconscious gesture she makes with her hair. Make your experience be all about that. As you drop away, so will your anxiety.

Isn't it astounding that when you drop away, your experience does not? In fact, it intensifies. This takes self-awareness. The previous scenario involved being aware of how you intrude into external action. This next one involves looking inside for what lies under our apparent self.

What Your Desires Are Hiding

Desires run us much of the time. Whether they're harmless or evil, desires control us more than we care to admit. Yes, even the most advanced Buddhist practitioners I've ever met are still enmeshed in desires. Desires 'R' Us. And, as the Buddha taught, when we're in the grip of a desire and can't get it, or aren't yet getting it, or got it but are worried about losing it, or got it and already have lost it, we suffer. We experience dukkha. *Voilà la condition humaine.* If this is how we are and how we're going to stay, how can we make this condition better? Here's a trick for going beyond desire inspired by spiritual coach and interfaith minister Philip Goldberg's book, *Roadsign: Navigating Your Path to Spiritual Happiness.*

When you're feeling a desire, which is now and always, go deeper. Look at the desire and ask if you can get to the feeling you hope it will give you without actually satisfying the desire. So, let's say you desire the absolutely fabulous new outfit you saw as you walked by the window displays at Vendre des Airs. You must have it! You'll be unhappy until then. And when you do have it, what will you be then? What will be your state when at last you've put on those fancy threads? Imagine that state. Try to inhabit it.

Then go deeper. Ask yourself what else could lead to that state. Doing so, you realize that the state is in fact independent of the desire you were focused on. You understand that many things could get you there, including some that are free, some that are entirely inside you. Often just the finding of the deeper desire for the state you want to reach relaxes the shallower desire for the object you thought would take you there.

By the way, relaxation of desire is something Sigmund Freud saw and taught, to the profound benefit of the world. When we see deeply—into our unconscious—we find that many of our conscious desires are not in themselves at all important to attain. They only stand in for other desires that we need to come to understand and accept. Understanding this loosens the ties between desire and happiness. In doing so, it loosens the ties between desire and unhappiness as well.

Readers who know something about Buddhism know that it tends to take a pretty dim view of desire. I mean, desire comes off as the bad guy in the Four Noble Truths. It's Number Two, the one that causes Number One, dukkha. You don't get much dimmer than that. In contrast, the solution I've been explaining reveals a different take on desire. My take remains in harmony with classic Buddhist teachings, but I don't take all desire at face value. Some desires symbolize others. Pursuing such desires always leaves us with dukkha. Seeing through them may lead us to insight. Insight may then allow us to pursue some desires with less attachment and more wisdom and compassion.

The Four Noble Truths teach that dukkha is the result of not getting or keeping our desires. Notice, though, that this does not mean desires are in themselves dukkha. It is only what we do with our experience of desire, not whether we get or keep it, that's dukkha. It's our experience we need to change, not desire itself. As I said, desires are us. We cannot honestly deny all of them. Instead, the honest path is to accept both desires and our lack of attaining them. One way to work toward that goal is the practice of looking beneath desires.

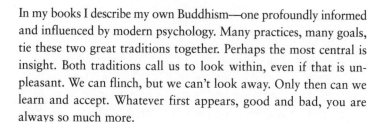

In my books I describe my own Buddhism—one profoundly informed and influenced by modern psychology. Many practices, many goals, tie these two great traditions together. Perhaps the most central is insight. Both traditions call us to look within, even if that is unpleasant. We can flinch, but we can't look away. Only then can we learn and accept. Whatever first appears, good and bad, you are always so much more.

I Am More Than This!

Here's a really short and simple technique, yet one you'll be able to use in a thousand situations.

 Suppose you're stuck in the rain, soaked and freezing. Say this phrase: "I am more than these feelings."

Suppose you're listening to someone chew you out and beginning to feel anger. Say this phrase: "I am more than these feelings."

Suppose that you're feeling homesick or even that you've lost someone you love. Say this phrase: "I am more than these feelings."

Say it aloud, if you can. If not, shut your eyes for those quick seconds it takes to say it. Focus your attention. Really mean it, if only for that brief moment. It will help.

As I say, there are a thousand opportunities to repeat this reminder of who you really are. Let yourself feel pain, anger, frustration, or boredom, but also know you are more than that. As Walt Whitman knew well, you are large, you contain multitudes.

There's an open quality we find in greatly wise persons. I call it "spaciousness." Great leaders, writers, lovers live in that inner spaciousness that always allows them to be "more than this." Such spaciousness also allows flexibility, the power to find the goodness in change, even when change is undesired.

When Things Don't Go According to Plan

We are constantly working on schemes to make our lives better. Some of us even work on schemes to make other people's lives better. And we're constantly finding that, no matter how brilliant our schemes and flawless their execution, they still often fail. There's no more painful example of this than marriage. Despite genuine love and the beautiful dreams of newlyweds, half of our marriages end in divorce. And the other half end in death.

More concretely, we face alteration in our plans and expectations every day. The bus is late to the airport, the rain comes down on your picnic, they're out of sourdough at the store. Sigh. When such things happen to me (which is every day), I try to remind myself that this is all beyond me. In doing so, I often use the words, not of Buddha, but of Shakespeare.

 Yes, Shakespeare has great things to teach us about life, love, and even spirit, as Jess Winfield has shown us in his book *What Would Shakespeare Do?* Here's one Shakespearean passage I repeat to myself when faced with inevitable change:

> Full fathom five thy father lies;
> Of his bones are coral made;
> Those are pearls that were his eyes:
> Nothing of him that doth fade
> But doth suffer a sea-change
> Into something rich and strange.

The Tempest, Act I, Scene 2

There's something "rich and strange" in these words themselves—in the way they transform the sorrow of loss into the treasures of the deep. Fate works its changes upon us and the thousand intricate plans that flesh gives birth to. Repeating Shakespeare's enduring poetry and wisdom gives me strength, knowing 'twas ever thus and that the sea-changes our lives suffer may not be wished and yet may enrich us all the same.

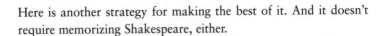

Here is another strategy for making the best of it. And it doesn't require memorizing Shakespeare, either.

You Think This Is Bad? Just Wait!

Suppose you are experiencing one of those everyday, ordinary annoyances we have all the time. If you think you've never had a problem like that, or haven't ever noticed one, you don't need the practice I'm about to teach you. How nice for you! But in case you're a *human being* and so do have problems now and then, here's a little something for you.

When you experience problems, putting them in context helps. Are you annoyed by, say mosquito bites? Damn, those things bug me! When you're lying in bed and you can't sleep because of the intolerable itching, here's what the Tibetan teacher Lama Zopa Rinpoche suggests you say: "This problem is like a great pleasure for me. There are much heavier problems to come."

Isn't that fabulous? I love this practice. It not only makes me feel less awful, sometimes it makes me laugh at myself, which is always good. Mosquito bites definitely suck, but mosquito bites are nothing compared to what awaits. I don't know what that may be; you don't either. But the point is, it's not happening now. If mosquito bites are your problem now, you're doing fine.

Why does this practice work so well? I believe it's because fantasizing the worst immediately makes reality much more bearable. Here's another trivial example. We do this with sports teams, envisioning the other team scoring a touchdown every play or making every three-pointer. When it doesn't happen, we feel better. Our team has got a chance. That's how we are about everything. After considering the worst-case scenario, the real-life scenario seems fine. This is true with everything.

Kurt Vonnegut tells an autobiographical story in his novel *Slaughterhouse Five* about his railway journey to a German POW camp. It was a terrible journey through the cold, without food. A hobo in Vonnegut's cattle car asked him if he thought things were bad. The hobo said he could be comfortable anywhere. Next day, the hobo died. Here are his last words: "You think this is bad? This ain't bad."

Perhaps you think that story's a bit morbid. I don't see it that way. I see it as a story of making the best of it. That hobo died as happy as he could be, because he kept thinking, right to the end, "This problem ain't bad." That hobo is a hero of mine. May we all live our lives so well! Whatever your problem, remind yourself this is nothin', this ain't bad. This is a piece of cake. Everything will be worse later. Right now I'm enjoyin' myself.

<hr />

Was that hobo in Vonnegut's cattle car a Buddha? A bodhisattva? We don't know. What we know is he died happy. We'd all be wise to settle for that.

Meanwhile, we've got work to do to set us up for that moment. I'm sure that others have noticed that Buddhist meditation is practice for death. We do it to let go of the self temporarily, so that when we need to let go permanently, we're ready (or as ready as we'll ever be). In a sense, all our life is this kind of practice or preparation. We must live well now so we can die well then.

I've been giving strategies for coping with problems and annoyances. But life is not always so annoying. In fact, life is more often simply dull. So I want to close this chapter with one solution to the dullness of existence, especially as perceived by us 21st century freaks.

When You Need a Soundtrack to Enliven Your Life

Life is not always terribly interesting when seen from our current, postmodern perspective. Our senses are fed a steady diet of "blooming buzzing confusion" far beyond what psychologist and philosopher William James saw 100 years ago when he coined that phrase. We've become so inured to this intensity of stimulation that we get bored when it slows down to a mere dull roar. We think, there's not enough! I need more! Give me more!

I suggest this is the wrong way to look at things. Life, as James knew, is overflowing with stimuli every moment. Almost at every second, we shut our senses down to reduce the input. We need to do this in order not to be constantly blown away by the intensity of every single instant we keep our eyes open. But as we practice living this way, we slowly lose the facility to really open our eyes when things slow down. So let me offer you another practice from Buddhist author Sumi Loundon. This is something we can do to liven things up—or, more literally, to liven our selves up:

> A trick I have when things are boring is to imagine the moment as if it were a movie moment, super nostalgic like, with lots of wistful or dramatic or emotional music. I think about how this particular combination of people, colors, sounds, motions, smells, etc. can never happen again. It's the only time I'll ever be able to witness this moment. That helps me to really appreciate even the super-crappy stuff, like fights and bad weather.

When you see a movie, you get carried away by it and don't notice the time passing. You are immersed in its reality, its moments, because it is heightened reality, complete with soundtrack. But if a movie can be that rich and engrossing and yet be simply light projected on a two-dimensional rectangle, then how much more engrossing can your real life be! Our lives have no soundtrack, but when we call to mind the fleeting nature of their moments, we find so much in them that we cannot be bored. I give life two thumbs up.

As Loundon says, this practice of thinking of life as a movie doesn't just work with boring moments; it can also help with nasty ones. Whatever is happening, is happening now and only now. When it passes away it will not return. This moment is our only chance to experience this unique, integral now. Every moment must pass away to make room for the next moment and the experiences it will bring. The more we open ourselves to the blooming of this moment, the more it comes alive just as it is, helping us both enjoy its pleasures and accept its pain—a good practice either way. So experience your life as a brilliant cinematic triumph. It's a goofy trick, but it's an award winner.

We've talked about the mind in this chapter. The mind is where it all happens. But as I said in the beginning, what happens in the mind affects what happens outside it. If we practice the skills and solutions this chapter provides, we can slowly change our minds. If we can do that, we can slowly change our worlds. Living in the world, and changing the world with skill, is the focus of the next chapter—the last and maybe toughest of them all. Don't worry. You're ready.

6

Things Larger Than You (Like, Say, the Universe)

THIS IS OUR FINAL CHAPTER, and, as the title says, here we tackle the big stuff, the universe, or, as the Buddhists call it, "the whole enchilada." (That's a very loose translation of "*paticca samutpada*," which it rhymes with.) Everything is bound together. In fact, everything only exists because of everything else and in everything else. That means that all our actions, even our thoughts, change the world. So this chapter offers solutions to problems we experience inside, but whose solutions also help outside.

First and most crucial is this fundamental change:

Coming to the End of Your Quest for Enlightenment (in One Minute)

I am sometimes deeply frustrated with my lack of spiritual progress. I meditate and I'm assailed by a thousand banal thoughts.

I'm trying to be a bodhisattva, but I find myself behind some jerk in the supermarket's "15 Items or Less" line with 23 items in his cart. I know this because I had to count them and now can't stop criticizing him in my mind. Or I'm attempting to live with spiritual intensity and yet staring at the turn signal someone has left on, missing the mountains hiding behind it. What's worse, when I catch myself at all this crap I get not only annoyed but really worried about my state. I'm growing older and not *getting* anywhere. I need a bolt of awakening quick, before I die! I need a huge breakthrough to give my life meaning. Maybe I should go on an extended meditation retreat and make some real progress. I've got to get away from my wife and my students and peace work and book writing and interfaith dialogue and really get into serious spiritual work. I need enlightenment!

When I feel this desire, which sometimes even approaches a kind of panic, I snap myself out of it by saying something like this:

 "Fuck spirituality.
Do better.
Love more."

Now that is sound advice, compassionate and wise. Notice how all that spirituality talk in that first paragraph was about *me*? There's something deeply dangerous in the self-centered pursuit of enlightenment. That pursuit can so easily devolve into something narcissistic and mean-spirited. For a few extraordinary folks, narrow spiritual goals benefit all living things. Their work blesses us. But, speaking for myself, over the years I've found that highfalutin' spiritual goals—especially the "Big E," Enlightenment (whatever that means)—have pretty much been an excuse for not doing better and loving more where it counts, in the real world.

So, though it sounds a bit drastic, go ahead, fuck spirituality. Instantly you're free to put that energy into doing better and loving more. The Buddha smiles.

Those of you who haven't thrown the book down in disgust know what I mean: real liberation is liberation *from* the self, not *in* the self. So a turn away from the "spiritual" and toward the "practical" is a turn for the better. Real practice leads to real results. This is why Jesus said of religious leaders, "By their fruits you shall know them." What fruits are we growing in our orchards? What karma is ripening on our trees? Let it be a harvest to feed the hunger of the world!

Okay then, while we're planting and watering and so on, how can we tell whether the fruits of these actions will be good ones? Buddhism gives us several standards. Here's a trick I use to see if I'm living up to them.

One Way to Tell Whether Doing Something Is Okay

There are times we're sorely tempted to do something dubious to get some sort of attached reward (pleasure, money, credit, whatever). At such times we're apt to think of very clever rationalizations. Don't think I don't know you know what I'm talking about. (If you know what I mean.)

Life is constantly offering us easy outs and sleazy cheats to get things we want. It might be as simple as pretending you baked the cookies you bought. Or perhaps letting everyone think you paid your dues, even though you didn't. Sometimes you don't even try to do such things, they just happen. But then there are those times you worry you really will try, when the temptation to steal a cupcake—or a kiss—is so strong you're on the edge of doing the easy thing you'll regret, later. As *Dhammapada* 244-245 points out,

Life is easy for the shameless, cunning,
Corrupt, brazen, nasty, and betraying.
But for one who's honest and insightful,
Trying to pursue purity, it's hard.

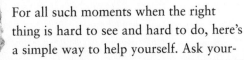 For all such moments when the right thing is hard to see and hard to do, here's a simple way to help yourself. Ask yourself "Am I cool with admitting this to my kid?" If yes, go ahead, you are in the clear. But if no, you can't do it. You know it, and this new awareness will help you resist.

You can do this even if you don't have a kid. Just imagine a young and impressionable child looking up at you with wide and trusting eyes. That kid does not understand the world and what to do in it. Imagine that he is looking for you to model himself on. He needs your example and your explanation to have a worthwhile life. Now go on, just what are you going to say to him? Explain yourself. And if you can't, then change.

In case the Buddhism in this answer is not obvious, here's what's going on. It's my way of leading myself back into awareness of my morality and responsibility to all things. That means it's a way of maintaining the Five Precepts, which are central to Buddhism. You may not see it at first, but, like every trick in this book, it grows from 2500 years of wisdom and practice. On one level, you're asking "What will my kid think?" On another you're asking "What would Buddha do?"

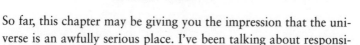 Bringing up the Buddha brings up another, more traditional, way to quickly guide our virtuous action. Instead of turning to your kid, turn to the Buddha. Visualize the buddha looking at you as you act. You act, he reacts. Is he smiling? Is he cocking an eyebrow? Is he turning away in disgust? Seeing the Buddha's reaction, you'll know if you're doing what he'd do, encourage, or allow. How does this make you feel? It makes you feel like doing good.

Making you feel like doing good is of course exactly what the Five Precepts are for. They don't prescribe behavior; they support practice. They guide us as we try to follow the middle way. Mahayana Buddhists add more, but here are the Five Precepts all Buddhists share:

1) trying not to kill, or even harm, things needlessly;
2) trying not to take what is not ours;
3) trying not to engage in harmful sex;
4) trying not to lie and harm through words; and
5) trying not to harm our minds with intoxicants.

This is now we acquire virtue and excellence. So simple; so vital.

So far, this chapter may be giving you the impression that the universe is an awfully serious place. I've been talking about responsibility and karma and morality. You're right, that's heavy stuff. But the universe is not always so heavy. We encounter things larger than ourselves all the time and one of the largest is also one of the freest and lightest: the Internet. The 'Net is really a symbol of the entire universe, every aspect of it linked together like Indra's Net.

> Indra's Net is a well-known Buddhist metaphor for the cosmos. The *Avatamsaka Sutra*, a central (and enormous) Mahayana text, describes the celestial abode of the god Indra, who's had fashioned an endless net in which each interstice holds a jewel with infinite facets, each face reflecting another jewel. Further, since each jewel thus reflects every other jewel, even each facet contains a reflection of all the others. In this way, Indra's entire net is contained in each of its parts and each part is directly connected to all the others. The sutra teaches that this is the nature of our universe.

Here are a couple solutions to problems we encounter in cyberspace.

Lighten up, of Course the URL Is Bad!

Whether you need that web site for work or for play, I know you get frustrated when it's not there anymore. I'm online all the time and find it exceptionally annoying when I've searched for some exact information and maybe found it, only to have my hopes dashed when I get that message, "404: Page Not Found." Here's a haiku from the Salon.com haiku computer error message contest:

> *You step in the stream,*
> *but the water has moved on.*
> *This page is not here.*

Cass Whittington

The World Wide Web is just like life, eh? It's always moving on. We don't really want to stop it, but we wish we could hold onto little bits of it. Faced with our ultimate conflict between the desire for permanence and the reality of change, we have to learn to embrace change. Let me quote another Salon.com haiku:

The Web site you seek
cannot be located but
endless others exist

Joy Rothke

When you can't find the page you want, remind yourself of this reassuring truth: endless others exist. In fact, when you feel that little surge of frustration and adrenaline, repeat it like a mantra, "endless others exist, endless others exist, endless others exist. . . ."

This is not only practical wisdom, it's profound wisdom. Ms. Rothke really tells us the truth here: we seek one thing we desire and treasure, yet the Web is full of endless other things. The secret to surfing the 'Net is to open ourselves to the endlessness of the thing. Page not there? Well, what is there? Look at that. The secret to life is not so different. We must open ourselves to the endlessness of experience. Every moment is rich beyond measure.

The Net Is Your Buddha Field

Ever wonder why people can be so hypersensitive and yet also so mean in e-mail? It's because e-mail, like a car, is an intrinsically dehumanizing place to connect with people. It takes away a whole dimension (in fact, *three* dimensions) of our lives. We cease to be fully human beings to each other. On the road, we become hard metal objects; on the 'Net, we become fleeting lines on a screen. No wonder we fail to really see and care for each other in these situations.

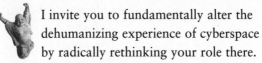 I invite you to fundamentally alter the dehumanizing experience of cyberspace by radically rethinking your role there. Instead of thinking of yourself as a text or a cipher and the vast expanse of everyone on the 'Net as faceless e-mail addresses, think of yourself as a powerful bodhisattva full of wisdom and compassion and all those other denizens of cyberspace as suffering beings in need of your help.

This may sound a bit grandiose, so let me buoy you up. The fundamental aspiration of hundreds of millions of Mahayana Buddhists around the world is to act exactly the way I've just described in real life. Now, doing this in real life is hard because we're always here and people need and ask a lot. By comparison, being a bodhisattva on the 'Net is relatively easy. After all, you're only online a few hours a day at most.

Hear the flames of others as cries of pain; take pity on them. Return their anger with cooling words of help. Let your fingers flow with wisdom and compassion! As you practice being a bodhisattva, your virtual powers will strengthen your real powers.

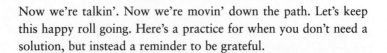

Now we're talkin'. Now we're movin' down the path. Let's keep this happy roll going. Here's a practice for when you don't need a solution, but instead a reminder to be grateful.

When Everything Is Just Totally Not Fucked Up

Naturally, in a book like this, there has to be a certain focus on misfortunes. But life is not entirely composed of troubles and tribulations, for goodness' sake. Sometimes life is good. Sometimes life is sweet. No need to give you examples of when this is so; you know it when you feel it. What I want to give you, instead, is a fun little practice you can do to help you enrich those times when all is well.

When life is smooth and precious, turn around the old, woeful plaint and ask the heavens "Why *me*? Why am I still alive and healthy? Why must I be happy? What did I do to *deserve* this?" You can ask these profound questions when you rise in the morning, when lay down at night, and anytime you realize your fortune. As you ask, whether in your head or out loud, you reinforce your feelings of gratitude and acceptance. Not only does this deepen your happiness now, it's vital practice for future times that may not be so easy.

You may not have a good answer to your questions. If you happen to have a good answer, keep it going. If you don't, simply be grateful. You don't need an answer, after all. You don't need to know why you're blessed. Just be grateful and radiate that gratitude out to the world.

The deeper practice here is compassion for all beings. Whether in joy or suffering, even though we don't fully understand the infinite machinery of the cosmos, we're all in this together. We're best off being humble, loving, kind, and accepting. Let your joy reflect back onto others. And when pain happens (as happen it must), accept it, hoping that others need not.

This is the basis of Tibetan *tonglen*, a lifelong practice of sending goodness out to others and taking on their misery. That's a little deeper, so I'll tell you more about it in the very last answer in the book. For now, we're just talking about what to do when life gives you joy. Ask "why me?" and let yourself smile at the strangeness of not knowing. There's no understanding it, only joyful acceptance. Share that freely.

Don't forget, we can always deepen our experience and sharing of life's blessings. When we accept life, really let it in, we can be grateful in more situations than we might imagine.

Okay, that's just about enough good feeling for one chapter. Time to get back to the main focus of this book: helping us through the hard parts of life. So here's something for both good and bad times.

When Your Cup Runneth Over: Making Offerings Every Moment

You no doubt have moments, as I do, when things just seem to be going great. Or when you maybe know in the back of your mind that things are great, yet you're just driving dully along and then, instead of just looking at the billboards, you look behind them and notice with shock and delight a glowing, burning, blazing sunset, clouds golden against the fading azure sky. Wow! You wish you could do something about it. You wish you could give it to someone. Well, *do* it.

Here are two practices on two levels. You can do both. On the human level, quick, call your partner! Tell them to get out on the balcony and look at the magnificent infinity of the sky. There, you have given this gift to someone.

On the cosmic level (which befits a moment like this), you can also offer this gift back to the infinite from which it came. As Taigen Dan Leighton writes in *Faces of Compassion*, we can offer the Buddha "a beautiful sunset, the drifting clouds, a field of wildflowers, a baby's smile, or our efforts to act with kindness." What a profound gift, and what a perfect and ever-present way to bring us closer to the sacred. You can't get much closer than when both the gift and the recipient are sacred. And these opportunities are constant. Even if you don't see a baby smile every day, you surely see *someone* smile, and I know you're trying to act with kindness.

Opportunities like this do not just happen during glorious heavenly events like sunsets (and sunrises, too, I'm told, though I don't generally enjoy being up to see them). I recently had quite a nasty editorial exchange. I thought I was fine until a colleague e-mailed me his support and I broke down in tears. It was as if he were Avalokiteshvara, hearing my inner cry and releasing it. (More on Avalokiteshvara in a few pages.) My hurt turned to profound gratitude for compassion and for mentoring. It was no longer hurt but liberating joy for what people can be and should be for each other. I offered my tears to all beings, knowing in that moment a compassion that encompassed them all.

Offerings can begin anywhere, with any emotion. Offer the Buddha your gratitude for life, your exhaustion, your crankiness, your breathing. There's no reason ever to stop.

Now I'm going to share with you a series of practices and empowerments that show the universality of the Buddha's wisdom. Instead of drawing on wisdom from the cultures of India or China, these draw on our Western culture, on the wisdom of our own teachers, and on our own personal wisdom—which is not separate from the Buddha's wisdom. Let's start by turning again to the greatest writer in the history of the English language: Shakespeare. There is both truth and beauty in his words and his characters.

"The Readiness Is All": The Wisdom of Hamlet, the Bodhisattva

Let me invite you to think of Hamlet as a bodhisattva, a being full of wisdom beyond the normal run of humanity, and a being torn by his need to right the wrongs of his kingdom. Once you can see Hamlet this way, you can learn from his example and his teaching.

Hamlet is of course a brilliant prince, thoughtful and eloquent. He, perhaps more than any other character in English literature, speaks for us in expressing the dilemmas of a moral and loving person placed in a truly horrible situation. Hamlet does not flinch, and by the end of the play he offers us this profound advice:

We defy augury; there's a special providence in the
fall of a sparrow. If it be now, 'tis not to come, if it be
not to come, it will be now; if it be not now, yet it will
come: the readiness is all. Since no man knows aught
of what he leaves, what is't to leave betimes? Let be.

Hamlet, Act V, Scene 2

Hamlet here sees his own upcoming death, yet turns to life. He
does not hide, nor does he quail. Hamlet acts. When he says none
of us "knows aught of what he leaves," he reminds us we forget life
at death and so should live life fully now. If we can truly do this,
we can die with dignity and forgiveness—as Hamlet does with ex-
traordinarily large grace.

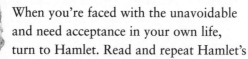 When you're faced with the unavoidable
and need acceptance in your own life,
turn to Hamlet. Read and repeat Hamlet's
words as a powerful mantra or the words of a
precious teacher, cutting to the heart of our lives
on this earth. When you know you will soon lose
something or someone you love, repeat Hamlet's
wisdom. You can choose any part of this passage or
the whole thing. Start with those last two syllables:
they form a particularly intense English mantra.

Hamlet's words accept what is, and—when we remember that
Hamlet then goes on to act—they also express what must be done.
This is what mantra practice is for: to orient us and empower us.
Moreover, the words of Shakespeare (along with the King James

Bible, which Hamlet echoes here) are as close to mantras as we come in our language.

Reading Hamlet's wisdom and compassion as he faces and lives out the end of his life end is like reading a Jataka tale, one of the stories of the Buddha before his last incarnation. In those stories, no matter who he is, even if he's an animal, the Buddha-to-be embodies the virtues of wisdom and compassion, just as Hamlet does. The Buddha-to-be's lives and deaths always teach lessons and, we hope, inspire us to follow his example. Hamlet does the same in finding and extending grace. Acting on his wisdom and in exchanging his forgiveness with his foe, Laertes, as they both die, Hamlet accepts what in Buddhism we call *anicca* (impermanence). Everything arises and falls away. An end comes to everything, if not now, it will come, and so "the readiness is all"; it is the key to our true ease and happiness. This makes Hamlet our teacher and his teaching a boon to us. Let be.

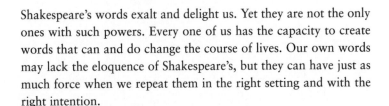

Shakespeare's words exalt and delight us. Yet they are not the only ones with such powers. Every one of us has the capacity to create words that can and do change the course of lives. Our own words may lack the eloquence of Shakespeare's, but they can have just as much force when we repeat them in the right setting and with the right intention.

Harnessing the Power of Vows

We imagine ourselves making vows in rare and specific situations. When we're getting married, for instance, or when we're taking religious ordination (which, of course, most of us never do). By contrast, those vowlike things we make at New Year's we don't call vows: we call them "resolutions." And we don't "take" them, we "make" them. Vows are different. They seem not to come from us; instead, we take them in, accepting them from outside. In taking vows we open up to something larger than ourselves, and we do this so seldom that vows remain extremely powerful motivators for us.

So, what are vows, really? Vows are conscious acts consisting of speech. Yes, speech is an act, and a speech can change things. Vows are words we put to our aspirations to change or grow. Harnessing the power of vows is one way to support these processes. When the minister asks whether you vow to have and to hold your partner, and you say "I do," the power of your vow supports your aspiration. Why not put some new words to some new virtuous aspirations?

Start small. Vow to be grateful throughout a meal. You don't need to be elaborate, after all, you're just vowing to do something for half an hour. No need to make a big production. Try just putting your hands together respectfully and saying, "I vow to remain grateful throughout this meal." Vow to smile at the next person who looks at you. Vow to root for your sports team with positive energy instead of moaning and swearing when they mess up. If that works, then perhaps vow to root for your work team with equal energy throughout a whole meeting. (Oh, yeah, this is tougher.) These are vows you can take and keep. As you do, your strength will grow.

When you've learned how vows can move you and inspire you in such everyday actions, you can

choose to take this practice further. The power of
small vows is brief but strong. The power of large
vows extends beyond ourselves. Consider the
power of vows you cannot keep but cannot forget. How about making an "impossible" vow, like
stopping global warming. You will not succeed in
this life, but is that so bad? Success is a process.
Vow to love your partner always. Vow to end
war. Vow to save all living things. It's a start.

The very words of vows have power. Their power lies in their per-
formative character. There is another kind of power words have,
independent of us: the power of their sounds. The English language
has been consciously unaware of this tradition of sound as power,
but the vitality of music shows us that the power exists. For those
of us who grew up in the '60s and '70s, mantras were central to
who we became. We didn't realize that Bob Dylan, Joni Mitchell,
John Lennon, Marvin Gaye, and Joe Strummer were bodhisattvas
dispensing mantras for the masses. But they were.

If such folks can make mantras, we can adopt them. We may
even think we can write our own. Perhaps so, or perhaps we'll just
be finding them. Either way. . . .

Make Your Own Mantras

Who says only dharma teachers and gurus can give mantras? Alright,
alright, the venerable wisdom of traditional Hinduism and Buddhism
says that. These traditional religions hold that voicing certain sounds
and phrases in Sanskrit (the ancient and sacred language of India)

gives rise to beneficial effects. Mantras in these traditions have been used to empower us on our spiritual paths, and only authorized teachers in such traditions should give out mantras designed to do this work. I won't argue about that, but here's a new thought. What if we considered other kinds of mantras for other kinds of paths? That doesn't infringe on the spiritual territory of gurus, but it may give rise to benefits we've yet to know. (Plus, after the first scenario in this chapter, you know how much I value "spiritual territory." The gurus can keep it.)

In fact, we're all constantly repeating mantras. It's just that they're secular ones, ones we don't recognize as mantras. Still, whether we recognize them or not, they have power over us. Consider these: "You're too fat." "Beat L.A.!" "Buy low, sell high." And if those weren't powerful enough for you, how about "God bless America," "The only good Indian is a dead Indian," and "My country, right or wrong!"? Let me repeat: mantras have power, political as well as emotional, negative as well as positive.

So far I've mentioned mantras that have been neutral at best, vile at worst. Our lives are full of such mantras. If you watch TV, you're force-fed a hundred a day. Mantras are operating on us all the time. Cultural mantras move us to do the things culture commands. These are not necessarily in our interest, but as we recognize the power of mantras, we can take that power back.

I encourage you to try out some better mantras. They're easy as pie to create. Hey, there's one now: "Easy as pie." You could repeat that in times of struggle. Seriously. But create your own. For example, I say "Every day is a good day" as a mantra. It's actually the last line of a Zen koan, but it works as a mantra on its own. I don't have to know why or how every day is a good day. I just repeat the phrase and let it be so.

The Zen tradition prides itself on "not relying on words and letters." Ironically, though, it's been dominated for a thousand years by elaborate traditions of questions and answers that involve memorizing sections of poetry and prose. Teachers ask students to "solve" koans, but answers to these and to follow-up questions are usually memorized answers called "capping phrases." They're also effectively mantras. See Victor Sogen Hori's book *Zen Sand* for literally thousands of them.

Here are a few ideas for mantras. I offer them because they are so everyday: "Thank you," "I love you," "Blessings." Or how about "I hear you," "You rock!" "Hell yeah!" whatever. Verbalize the positive. This may be the easiest trick in the book once you get the hang of it.

Before we forget about the '60s, I'm going to reach back to them once more. Don't worry, this trick does not depend on remembering that ancient decade. In fact, this solution to problems goes quite a lot farther back than that.

A Prayer We All Can Use (and One for the Sixties Generation)

When trouble mounts to the point of actual danger, we may feel powerless and terrified. This is natural. It is also inevitable, for no one avoids accidents and tragedies in this life. When trouble finds us, we must not add to it by criticizing ourselves, even if we have helped bring on the trouble. Instead, in the very moment of danger, we need to stay as open and positive as possible. It's very difficult, but prayer can help.

Did you think prayer had no place in a Buddhist book? Do Buddhists actually pray? Yes, of course Buddhists pray, why wouldn't they? Think of it this way. Do Christians pray only to God? Of course not. In fact, many pray to saints, spirits of benevolence who remain close to living things, giving them aid in times of need. That description fits bodhisattvas perfectly as well. They too are benevolent beings who remain in this world to aid sentient beings in times of need. Perhaps the greatest of these beings is Avalokiteshvara, the bodhisattva of compassion, the one "who hears the cries of the world." I've mentioned him, or her, before. Being so important, this bodhisattva has many names in many countries, and also many forms, both male and female. How can Guanyin be a woman and Avalokiteshvara be a man and both of them be the same bodhisattva? Because a being like this wants so very much to be there for us in all the ways we need. This is why Avalokiteshvara is often shown with a thousand heads and a thousand arms—the better to see us and aid us when we call.

The current Dalai Lama, Tenzin Gyatso, the fourteenth to hold the title, powerfully supports the belief that every Dalai Lama is an incarnation of Chenrezig. Through his long struggle against the Chinese occupiers and destroyers of his country, he has shown patience and compassion unsurpassed in our time. He truly embodies the compassion of Chenrezig. That's why he has become a Buddhist celebrity and why he has been honored with the Nobel Peace Prize, perhaps the greatest honor in this world. And that's why, in my own life, I feel so blessed to have looked in his eyes as we bowed to each other many years ago. That fleeting moment, lost in a sea of such moments for him, remains vivid and deeply meaningful to me and always will. Such is the power in the man.

In times of danger, pain, strife, and confusion, we can pray to Avalokiteshvara, to Kanzeon, to aid us. The Lotus Sutra is full of examples of such prayers and testimonies to the miraculous power of the bodhisattva to save us from our troubles. I've never been in a situation where I had to throw my whole future into the hands of Kanzeon. Still, I'd like to think I could and that that it couldn't hurt. In the meantime, we can use the closing verse of the Kanzeon chapter of the *Lotus Sutra* as a prayer when we need it. It doesn't have to only be in life-and-death moments. Kanzeon is there to empower us all the time. We can call on her aid when we're lost on the road, when we're grieving over a loss, when we're cold and lonely, or when we just need a friend.

So when you're car breaks down in the rain, or you're about to take a seat in the dentist's chair, or you can't see how you're going to get back down the mountain in the dark, repeat these words from Taigen Dan Leighton's translation:

> *Eyes of compassion, observing sentient beings,*
> *assemble an immeasurable ocean of blessings.*

In the *Lotus Sutra*, this invocation can save us from fire, drowning, violence, poison, all the horrors of death. Surely it can ease your pain at the dentist's. And, if you're really in trouble, don't worry about the whole verse, just cry "Kanzeon!" and feel comforted.

Who is hearing? Who can aid you? Who is Kanzeon? I've told you the traditional answers to these questions. Do I claim to know the truth about the ontological status of Kanzeon? I don't. I am still in the dark. I know only this: when I cry out, I feel better crying to Kanzeon than cursing my darkness.

 And, having brought up all those "Who" questions, I'll add something for those in "my generation." You can call out to Kanzeon in many ways. If Kanzeon hears the cries of the world, she surely doesn't shut her ears to new cries in new words. For this reason, I think one perfect cry is "See me, feel me, touch me, heal me." How simple and yet how complete is this cry! May Kanzeon see, feel, touch, and heal us all.

You may have noticed that as we've gotten deeper into these "things larger than you," the tricks I offer have gotten deeper as well. That's right, I've been building up to this. Yes, they are quick solutions and fundamental ones, but if you build the foundation deep enough, you eventually reach profound depths. And if you don't feel you've quite gotten there (and who has?), at least you know you're building your house on bedrock.

Keeping in mind both enduring depth and the momentariness of experience, I offer two final practices for enriching yourself and the world. Both grow from and honor the interconnectedness of all things.

The Power of Unknowing

Admit that you don't know the answers. At work, when a subordinate asks you a question, don't know the answer. Ask her for her own ideas. When a supervisor asks you a question, don't know the answer. Learn from her experience about the subject. At home, when your partner asks why you're angry or what you can do together to deepen your relationship, don't know the answer. Discover it together. In politics, if you're perplexed by war, poverty, injustice, it's probably easy to admit you really don't know what to do, but take it farther. Say "I don't *know* what is wrong. I don't *know* who to vote for. I don't *know* how to fix things." This "I don't know" mind is powerful.

There's a wonderful story about Bodhidharma, the legendary Indian monk who brought Dhyana Buddhism (the meditation-centered school) to China. (It was later called Chan in China, Seon in Korea, Thien in Vietnam, and Zen in Japan.) In the story he is summoned to an audience with Emperor Wu, who has heard of Bodhidharma's great wisdom and miraculous feats. Long a proponent of Buddhism, the emperor has built temples and supported monks and so on. He's proud of this work, so he starts the conversation by mentioning his many good deeds, hoping perhaps to get on Bodhidharma's good side.

Now, Bodhidharma is a pretty quiet guy, so he doesn't say anything, and Emperor Wu, seeking a good starting place for their talk, asks him a direct question: "I have built all these temples and paid for all these ordinations of monks. What merit do you think I've made?"

Bodhidharma replies, "None at all."

This bugs the emperor, as you might expect, but trying to be a good Buddhist, he figures perhaps Bodhidharma is subtly chiding him for being proud. So Emperor Wu takes another tack, not talking about himself. Instead he asks a nice, simple question about the Buddha's teaching to give Bodhidharma a chance to show off his wisdom. Perhaps he's really curious, having thought up to now that his imperial Buddhism should be all about supporting the sangha. If that was incorrect, he wants to know what Buddhism really is about. So he asks, "What is the first principle of the dharma?"

And Bodhidharma answers, "Vast openness, no holiness."

By this point Emperor Wu is getting slightly peeved at this terse monk who will not play the game with him. After all, he's Wu, the Son of Heaven, Emperor of the Middle Kingdom, center of the world and pinnacle of all civilization, and this impudent monk is just a barbarian from the West. At that time China truly was the greatest civilization on earth—the largest, the most technologically advanced, the most literate and educated. Most Chinese, especially the elite, thought "Westerners," meaning people from India, with their gross red or brown hair, bulging round eyes, and bestial beards, were almost subhuman. So Emperor Wu is thinking "who the heck does this dirty punk of a monk think he is, talking to me like that?" He sternly demands, "Who is this person confronting me?"

And Bodhidharma answers, "I don't know."

It's said that this comment so disarmed Emperor Wu that he let Bodhidharma go. As I read it, Bodhidharma's not knowing saved not only his skin but, according to legend, the whole Zen dharma which he transmitted to others after his audience.

I want to encourage all of us to cultivate the power of Bodhidharma, the power of unknowing. The beloved Zen Teacher Shunryu Suzuki Roshi spoke of this unknowing as "beginner's mind." He also spoke of it as "Zen mind." No difference, no limitation.

Simply admitting you don't know makes room for learning, the center of our path in the world. On a practical level, honesty allows the opportunity for others to help you. People like to be owed when the person who owes is grateful. When you graciously owe another, you have an alliance with them. They know they can count on you in the future. (Indeed, putting my professor of religion hat on, I'll tell you this kind of reciprocal bond was the central form of currency in pre-capitalist cultures. It still is in local cultures around the world, and it is often tied to and enacted in religious values and rituals.)

On a deeper level (or higher level, choose your metaphor) unknowing is an opening to what is larger than yourself, what is bigger than your brain. Unknowing is an opening to the sacred. Let it in.

You might ask me, as a professor of religion, what is "the sacred?" Can you guess what I'm going to answer? I'll bet you can: I don't know! I'm letting it in.

 So here, again, is the practice: just say "I don't know." Nothing to it. You can practice this everywhere. I try to practice it all the time. As a teacher and author, I get asked a lot of questions, and people expect me to know the answers. But to say "I know" is to close the door to change and growth—not only mine, but that of my students and readers. To keep learning and growing, I can't already know the answers; nei-

ther can you. We can only come up with our
guesses and approximations, share them, and constantly try to be open to reshaping them, letting
them go, replacing them.

Learning from life is just like classroom learning. Admitting
that you don't know opens your mind to knowledge. Say "I don't
know," and be ready to learn. Unknowing is the first step to finding solutions. It is also the last step in embodying solutions, as
Bodhidharma showed.

This does not mean playing dumb. Unknowing is not the same
as unthinking. Unknowing gets you to a place of real openness,
but you still need to choose and act with intelligence and conviction. In Section 17 of *The Jewel Ornament of Liberation*, Gampopa
quotes the legendary Indian saint and philosopher Saraha's brilliant version of how not to be unknowing:

Those who hold to things are dumb as cows;
Those who hold to emptiness are even dumber.

Real unknowing is holding to neither and enjoying both.

If we don't know what to do, what do we do? That is a bit of a
conundrum, to be sure. ("To be sure"—ha! I hope you appreciate
that irony.) What shall we do tomorrow? What shall we ever do? I
have an answer for you. It's the last trick in the book, my final answer. You can pull it out and use it any time, anywhere. Start small
with it and expand it to the end of space and time. You can do it
right now, while you're reading, or you can save it for a rainy day
or a moment of ecstasy. Tibetan Buddhists have focused on it, but

it's fundamental practice for all Buddhists, everywhere, because it follows directly from the Buddha's central insight: that there's no essential difference between "me" and "everyone else." If there's no difference, then my sorrows are their sorrows, my joys their joys. And if that is so, then can I not share my joy and relieve their sorrow? Yes, we all can. Here's how.

Giving Pleasure, Taking Pain, Transforming the World

Pleasure and pain are the basic states of being in the world. We are all feeling either pain, pleasure, or a mixture of the two. These states of being offer us a constant field of practice for transforming the world. Let me start with an example and then explain it, since this is pretty deep stuff.

Let's say you have a headache. You realize your head aches. You perceive this pain. There are several things you can do with the pain. First, you can take aspirin, give yourself a little head massage, shut your eyes—whatever you can to relieve the pain. This is already a kind of Buddhist practice: you are seeing your painful state and taking action to change it. Very good.

 But while you're doing this, still in pain, you can also work with it on another level. You can accept it in the wider context of other beings as well as yourself. You can think of the pain as coming to you and not others. As long as you have it, they don't. As long as you experience it, they don't have to. When you experience pain, think "Experiencing this pain, may I relieve the pain of others." This is a way to turn trouble into a gift. As a mother sacrifices for her children and feels no conflict, so you can sacrifice for all beings. This may be easier if you believe, as the Tibetans do, that in previous lives all beings have been your children or your mother who sacrificed for you. Of course your pain remains pain, but it is transfigured through this process of accepting it to help others. Practicing this way, we benefit ourselves, as well. We benefit because we come to like trouble and so it naturally transforms to ease.

We're not all ready for this grand practice, heaven knows, at least not all the time. So start small; start by just accepting pain—already an excellent beginning. When life gives you pain, accept it without judgment. Then, if you can, strive to think of your having this pain so others will not. That way you can transmute your pain, turning the lead of suffering to the gold of transformation. It's really not that hard, since it doesn't cost you anything. In fact, it gives meaning to your pain. You can feel good even while you feel bad.

What I'm describing here is *tonglen* practice, the engine of Vajrayana Buddhism, the Diamond Vehicle. When bad things happen, think "How lucky I am to be able to do this tonglen practice. It's working: the pain of others has come to me, has ripened upon me." This is tough when the suffering seems intentional. Again start small.

Start with simple physical pain, like a headache. Headaches don't usually make you angry, so they give you an easy starting place to practice tonglen. Then you'll be better able to practice when serious problems come up, when you are tempted to be angry. Anger won't help decrease your pain; in fact, it will increase it. So practice now for those later times when the pain you feel is intentionally inflicted.

This is only half of the practice, of course. Tonglen doesn't just work with pain, it works with pleasure as well. When pleasure comes to you, offer that pleasure to all beings—just the reverse of the way you work with pain. As you take the pain from others, so you give your pleasure to others. When life gives you joy, share it with the world. You may share it practically in a smile, a hug, an e-mail, a gift, a good deed. You may share it prayerfully, radiating your joy to all living things. As you're moved, share joyfully.

Vajrayana Buddhism teaches that tonglen works through karma, the universal law of cause and effect. Karma lies at the root of all processes and expands, bad or good, as we work with it and amplify it. When we take in pain or give out pleasure, we exchange the roles of self and other. Doing this, we expand the good karma at work between ourselves and others. There are no losers when we play like this. In exchanging self and other, in this play of karma, suffering is turned to happiness, and happiness is multiplied.

We cease to be part of the problem. In fact, we cease even to be apart *from* the problem. We become part of the solution, and that's where I will leave us for now.

Just Add More

I CAN HARDLY LET YOU GO without further directions on the path. So here are a few of my greatest hits of sources for deeper information on Buddhism and on living life well.

Buddha

You can find many narratives of the Buddha's life on the net. These are a start, but they're relatively short and each is marked by the perspective of the Buddhist school that put the narrative there. So if you want to really learn something about the Buddha, his world, and his teaching, check out Karen Armstrong's *Buddha* (Penguin, 2001). Ms. Armstrong tries to separate fact from myth and to provide an introduction to the Buddha's teachings as near as we can come to them. She succeeds admirably.

For a really different take on the Buddha's life, check out the graphic novel series, *Buddha*, published by Vertical Press. Yes, that's right, the Buddha as comic book hero. And why not? Originally published in Japan by Osamu Tezuka, the father of manga, there'll be eight of them by the time they're done and they're coming out now with beautiful versions in English. Whether you're a scholar or a skinhead, I bet you'll like them.

Dharma

For the pure heart of Buddhism—the practice of mindfulness right now—please read Steve Hagen's *Buddhism Plain and Simple* (Tuttle, 1997). Yes, Hagen makes it plain and simple, and you can't do better than that. To immerse yourself in the vibrant ocean of Buddhism, try Roger Corless's *The Vision of Buddhism* (Paragon House, 1989). Scholar and practitioner Corless sees Buddhism for what it is, in all its variety and wonder. This is a wonderful place to begin further exploration. And, for a thorough but fun drive-by of Buddhist history and practice, Gary Gach's *Complete Idiot's Guide to Understanding Buddhism* (Alpha, 2004) is a great resource.

The Theravada Buddhist path is well-summed up in Bhante Henepola Gunaratana's *Eight Mindful Steps to Happiness* (Wisdom, 2001). Here Bhante (that means "venerable monk") Gunaratana lays out the whole eightfold path from a lucid, balanced, and traditional perspective.

Mahayana Buddhism is so complex and varied, no one book can fully describe it, but Taigen Dan Leighton's *Faces of Compassion* (Wisdom Publications, 2003), which I've mentioned before, is wondrous. Leighton, a scholar, a Zen teacher, and an activist, shows how the rich world of Mahayana bodhisattvas, their virtues, and the practices associated with them is our world. In so doing, he brings Mahayana profoundly to life and profoundly into our lives.

On Vajrayana Buddhism (a.k.a. Mantrayana Buddhism, Tantric Buddhism, and Tibetan Buddhism), try starting with the work of His Holiness the Dalai Lama (HHDL for short). He's not the foremost spiritual leader of all Tibetan Buddhists, Nobel Prize winner, and one of the most respected people in the entire world for nothing. HHDL has written many books on his own tradition, on psychology and Buddhism, on being happy, etc. Check out any one of them.

Since I love Zen, here are some Zen books for you. Robert Aitken's *Taking the Path of Zen* (North Point Press, 1982) introduces Zen so you can do it yourself. Aitken Roshi always writes with grace and clarity; all his books are valuable reading. For a compelling view of Zen practice, read Shunryu Suzuki's *Zen Mind, Beginner's Mind* (Weatherhill, 1970). It's a classic, especially if you're just starting out.

My favorite Buddhist autobiography is the story of Janwillem van de Wetering, a Dutchman who goes to Japan to live in a Zen monastery, then comes to America. He's written a trilogy filled with tough humor and nary a pulled punch. Lose your illusions and read *The Empty Mirror, A Glimpse of Nothingness*, and *Afterzen* (St. Martin's Press). And, if you like Zen humor, read David Chadwick's extremely funny account of his Buddhist and non-Buddhist experiences in Japan: *Thank You and OK!* (Penguin Arkana, 1994).

And now, a new kind of source for just adding more Buddha:

http://www.jbeonlinebooks.org/

This is the website where you can buy and download *Buddhism—the eBook* and *Buddhism: The American Experience*. Are they books, are they docs, are they sites? Who cares. The important thing is that if you're looking for the most up-to-date scholarly yet friendly information on Buddhism in history or Buddhism in America, here it is. These eBooks are written by scholars who know their stuff and who understand the future of information: it's online. These books not only provide their own information, they link you to all sorts of other sites for more. A great way to learn, especially if you don't live in a big city.

Sacred Texts

In this book, I've quoted text from throughout the ocean of Buddhism. Here are some places you can dive into parts of the ocean, yourself, and come up with your own favorites.

Many of the most important suttas from the *Pali Canon* are online at www.accesstoinsight.org/canon/. The site also includes other writings, like the *Dhammapada*, which I quote so often. The writings of the *Pali Canon* are central to Theravada Buddhism, but in slightly different versions they're vital to Mahayana Buddhism as well. Access to Insight is *the* place to begin a serious exploration of Buddhist texts.

Mahayana texts, including Zen and Vajrayana texts, are a bit tougher to find. Here are four good starting places:

http://www4.bayarea.net/~mtlee/

http://www.quangduc.net/English/Maha/

http://www.buddhanet.net/ (go to "file library/resources" and "eBook library")

http://www.ciolek.com/WWWVL-Buddhism.html (go to the Pure Land, Tibetan, and Zen "Virtual Library" pages)

Naturally, you can also find and read printed books. Your local library should have copies of the major Buddhist sacred texts, or at least excepts from them in collections. Some of my favorites are the

Lotus Sutra and the *Vimalakirti Sutra* (especially Burton Watson's translations); Shantideva's beautiful *Bodhicharyavatara* ("Way of the Bodhisattva"); the lovely Pure Land text, the *Tannisho*, by Shinran; and the central Zen texts, the *Record of Lin-chi* (translated by Watson again [Shambhala, 1993]), and the collection *Moon in a Dewdrop* by Dogen Zenji (translated and edited by Kazuaki Tanahashi [North Point, 1985]).

Sanghas

To find sanghas far and wide or near your home, here are the three best starting places:

www.dharmanet.org

This site has an analytical quality and excellent links to a huge range of study sites. Great for learning about various forms of Buddhism and their history. This site has the best links to U.S. meditation centers.

www.buddhanet.net

This one has a slight Theravada emphasis, is best for non-USA readers, annotates links nicely, and organizes itself more around practices and traditions. Great for learning about Theravada traditions, including many forms of meditation.

www.tricycle.com

This site is the online presence of the slick-but-good Buddhist magazine, *Tricycle*. It looks much better than the other sites and has a U.S. focus.

Gone, Gone, Gone Beyond, All Gone Beyond

There are more Buddhist websites than the mind can contain. This is wonderful if you're not near a sangha or a library. These days, it seems like every little meditation center or temple has its own website, and, of course, huge schools and institutions do, as well. The ones I list below are just a few of my favorites. Go find your own.

www.accesstoinsight.org

I've already mentioned this one. The best source for Theravada scriptures. It also gives solid meditation instructions and other guides for practice. On the traditional side.

www.buddhajones.com

This is by far the funniest Buddhist site I've ever seen. It's consistently provocative and topical. It's also creatively visual. Not on the traditional side!

www.kagyu.org

An excellent and thorough Vajrayana site. Of course, it's focused on Kagyu teachings, but it gives good background on all Tibetan Buddhism and some unusually detailed introduction to meditation practices.

www.robertaitken.net

Robert Aitken Roshi, an elder statesman of American Zen, is also a powerful writer and activist. This site includes many of his talks and writings and gives the flavor of this feisty and venerable teacher.

www.bpf.org

The Buddhist Peace Fellowship is devoted to increasing the peace and decreasing the dukkha of this world. They are the good guys.

www.syzenart.com

Song Yoon, a Korean monk, did the paintings in my last book, *Buddha in Your Backpack*. On his site you get a rest from words and see the clarity and beauty of his vision of the world. Be there!

www.mind2mind.net

My site. I've got Buddhist politics and humor you won't find anywhere else, plus links, my latest doings, and who-knows-what-all that didn't yet exist at press time.

Links are always changing—yes, like everything in the cosmos, just a little faster—for updates to the list below, go to www.mind2 mind.net/bdtlinks.html/.

Other Great Books

I mentioned these books in the text because they're useful in my life. Technically they're not about Buddhism, but they're also not separate from the path.

Gary Thorp, *Sweeping Changes: Discovering the Joy of Zen in Everyday Tasks* (Broadway, 2001). Revolutionize your relationship with dirt (inside and out).

Rachel Harris, *20-Minute Retreats: Revive Your Spirit in Just Minutes a Day with Simple, Self-Led Practices* (Owl Books, 2000). Yes, you really can.

Philip Goldberg, *Roadsigns: Navigating Your Path to Spiritual Happiness* (Rodale, 2003). Travel tips from a man who's been there and back.

Judie O'Neill and Bridget Fonger, *The Lazy Woman's Guide to Just About Everything: Practical Tips and Lazy Wisdom for a Life of Ease* (Elephant Eye Press, 2001). They are not kidding about "practical," and you know how much I respect that.

Glossary

Bodhisattva: literally, "awakening being"; a person who works to achieve liberation with and for all living beings, sometimes powerful and cosmic, sometimes us. Examples of celestial bodhisattvas are Avalokiteshvara, bodhisattva of compassion; Manjushri, bodhisattva of wisdom; Samantabhadra, bodhisattva of action; Kshitigarbha (popular as Jizo), bodhisattva protecting the weak; and Maitreya, the bodhisattva who will be the next Buddha here on earth.

Buddha: "awakened one"; there are many, including the historical Buddha, Shakyamuni; Amitabha or Amida, the Buddha of the Western Pure Land; and Vairochana, the celestial Sun Buddha; the first of Buddhism's Three Jewels.

Buddha Nature: the inherent potential in all beings to become Buddhas; also perhaps the underlying nature of all of us, right now.

Compassion: sympathy and love for all living things; one of the two principle Buddhist virtues (the other is wisdom).

Dharma or *Dhamma:* truth, the teaching of the Buddha; the second of the Three Jewels of Buddhism.

Dukkha: "dissatisfaction," "frustration," "unhappiness," or "suffering"; the existential pain we all have, caused by our attachment to fulfilling desire.

Eightfold Path: the Buddhist way of life; synonymous with "Middle Path" and "Middle Way."

Engaged Buddhism: a phrase coined by the monk Thich Nhat Hanh, naming the form of Buddhism that integrates wisdom and compassion into all aspects of life, including politics and the environment.

Five Precepts: the basics of Buddhist morality—1) not harming through violence, 2) not harming through stealing or hoarding, 3) not harming through sex, 4) not harming through words, 5) not harming through drugs.

Four Great Vows: bodhisattva vows taken and repeated by Mahayana Buddhists—1) living beings are numberless, I vow to save them; 2) desires are inexhaustible, I vow to abandon them; 3) dharma gates are countless, I vow to enter them; 4) the Buddha way is unsurpassable, I vow to embody it.

Four Noble Truths: Buddha's core teaching—1) life is full of dukkha (see above); 2) dukkha is caused by ignorance, desire, and attachment; 3) dukkha can end; 4) we end it through following the Buddhist path.

Jataka: a story of a past life of the being who would become Shakyamuni; collected into a set of moral tales, especially popular as teachings for children.

Karma: the law of cause and effect, especially as applied to our acts with our body, speech, and mind. These acts lead to outcomes in this life and possibly in others.

Lama: an incarnation of a Tibetan spiritual teacher or guru; the two most famous are the Dalai Lama and the Panchen Lama.

Mahayana: literally, "The Greater Vehicle"; the dominant form of Buddhism in East Asia, focused on striving for the awakening of all living things.

Mantra: a sacred sound or series of sounds repeated to generate merit, concentrate or clear the mind, and empower the person; an example is the last line of the Heart Sutra: "Gate, gate, paragate, parasamgate, bodhi svaha!" (Note: "gate" is pronounced "gah-tay.")

Meditation: practices of calming the mind (samatha meditation) and looking inward (vipassana meditation); Buddhism contains many types, traditionally done to help achieve awakening; last part of the Eightfold Path.

Nirvana: peace, ease; liberation from samsara (the universe).

Om Mani Padme Hum: a Sanskrit mantra with no literal meaning; the most popular mantra in Tibet; repeated to clear the mind and generate good karma.

Pure Land: the land of Amida Buddha where awakening is easy; millions of Buddhists pray to be reborn there.

Roshi, Sensei, Zenji: titles for Japanese Zen teachers.

Samsara: this dukkha-filled cosmos where living things are born, live, and die.

Sangha: the community of Buddhists; can mean monks and nuns only, or everyone on the path; the third of the Three Jewels of Buddhism.

Shakyamuni Buddha: literally "The Sage of the Shakya clan, the Awakened One"; Born Gautama Siddhartha; a real person; the historical Buddha.

Sutra or Sutta: an oral teaching of the Buddha, hundreds were eventually written down and collected; together they form the main sacred texts of Buddhism.

Theravada: literally "The Way of the Elders"; the dominant form of Buddhism in South and Southeast Asia; focused on striving for the awakening of monks and nuns.

Three Jewels of Buddhism: Buddha, dharma, and sangha; also called "The Three Treasures."

Vajrayana: literally "The Diamond Vehicle"; the dominant form of Buddhism in the Himalayas, especially Tibet; a variant of Mahayana Buddhism focused on striving for awakening in a single lifetime.

Wisdom: an understanding of the nature of reality; beyond intellectual knowing; one of the two principle Buddhist virtues (the other is compassion).

May you travel your path with good cheer and good companions!